Martinès de Pasqually

His Life – His Magical Practices – His Work – His Disciples

Available from Triad Press

PAPUS:

Exegesis on the Soul: Three Treatises on the Nature, Origin, & Destiny of the Human Soul
How to Read Hands: First Elements of Chiromancy
What a Master Mason Ought to Know
What is Occultism?

RELATED TITLES:

Abbé Julio: His Life, His Work, His Doctrine by Robert Ambelain
Apostolic Church of the Pleroma Clergy Handbook by Tau Phosphoros
The Arcane Schools by John Yarker
The Baylot Manuscript in Translation: BnF FM⁴15
Translated, Annotated, & Introduced by Sâr Phosphoros
Grand Marvelous Secrets by Abbé Julio
The Little Religions of Paris by Jules Bois
Masonic Orthodoxy: Followed by Occult Masonry and Hermetic Initiation by Jean-Marie Ragon
Occultist Freemasonry in the 18th century and the Order of Élus Coëns by René Le Forestier
The Pleromic Light Unveiled: An Instructive Monograph on the Holy Gnostic Liturgy of the Pleromic Light by Tau Phosphoros

ILLUMINISM IN FRANCE
1767-1774

MARTINÈS DE PASQUALLY

HIS LIFE - HIS MAGICAL PRACTICES - HIS WORK - HIS DISCIPLES

FOLLOWED BY
THE CATECHISM OF THE ÉLUS COËNS
ACCORDING TO SOME ENTIRELY UNPUBLISHED DOCUMENTS

by
PAPUS

Translated and introduced by
Sâr Phosphoros
Sovereign Grand Commander
Christian Knights of Saint-Martin

Fox Lake, IL

Martinès de Pasqually: His life, his magical practices, his work, his disciples.
by Papus (1895)

Translated and introduced by Sâr Phosphoros

First English edition
Published 2024

ISBN: 978-0-9973101-6-0

Triad Press, LLC
123 S. US Highway 12 #33
Fox Lake, IL 60020

TO MY FRIEND

VITTE

Engineer, old student of the Polytechnic School

To the Apostle of Unity

I dedicate this summary of the efforts of Martinès

Papus.

Depasqually delatour

THE SIGNATURE OF MARTINÈS
(Photograph from a manuscript)

TABLE OF CONTENTS

SEAL PLACED AT THE HEAD
OF THE MAJORITY OF THE LETTERS
OF MARTINÈS DE PASQUALLY

TRANSLATOR'S INTRODUCTION

In this work, Papus, co-founder with Augustin Chaboseau of the Ordre Martiniste and bishop of the Église Gnostique Universelle, attempts an analysis of the life and teachings of Martinès de Pasqually, founder of the Chevaliers Maçons Élus Coëns de l'Univers. The Élus Coëns was an 18th century Masonic rite little known in America today, but quite influential in the development of Freemasonry in France. The Élus Coëns was not just a Masonic rite, however, it was also a school of practical theurgy or ceremonial magic. It therefore existed in two worlds: the Masonic milieu of the bourgeois and the aristocracy vying for power and position in the fraternity; and the world of occultists and Kabbalists, often dominated by charlatans and would-be alchemists. From Pasqually's school emerged several gifted personages of both camps. Some of his "emulators" (the word he used to designate his disciples) would go on to great prominence in the Masonic world, helping to shape the future of French Masonry; while others, such as the celebrated Philosophe Inconnu, Louis-Claude de Saint-Martin, would abandon the Masonic system altogether for a more pure mysticism, dubbed the "inner way" or "way of the heart" as opposed to the "exterior way" or "operative way" of the Élus Coëns.

Papus conducts his study through the examination of numerous letters between Pasqually and his chief students, most notably, Jean-Baptiste Willermoz, head of the Order in Lyon. Some other authors have accused Papus of not understanding the intents and means of Pasqually and his school, or of superimposing his own agenda. It is true that Papus commits some errors and perhaps betrays some prejudices. One such error is his interpretation of "R.+" in the documents as "Rose-Croix" rather than "Réau-Croix" which was the actual title of the ultimate degree of the Order. This is an easily made oversight, however, and does not pose any significant change in meaning to the documents. It is entirely likely, moreover, that Pasqually intended for Réau-Croix to bring to mind the Rose-Croix. Papus' Masonic classifications, however, can be a little confusing until we understand his terminology. He refers to the Scottish or "Écossais" degrees collectively as the "Templar Rite." He justifies this by pointing out the general theme of Templar vengeance that runs through many of the degrees. But when it comes to an actual Templar rite, the Strict Observance, he refers to it as Illuminism or the Illuminati - not an incorrect designation, but nevertheless a little disorienting when contrasted with the so-called Templar Rite. But as long as one is able to keep his denominations straight - which he does more or less clearly define for us - the reader should not have much trouble following.

Papus does us the great favor of cleaning up much of Pasqually's horrific spelling, but he leaves us nevertheless with his unusual and sometimes nearly incomprehensible grammar and sentence constructions. We have done our best to provide a translation that walks the line between comprehension and preserving the peculiar quality of Pasqually's use of language. For example, there is one section where a part of a letter goes on for two straight pages without any punctuation, save a couple of randomly placed commas. In a circumstance such as this, we felt it necessary to break up the text into its natural divisions, using standard punctuation. However, when it comes to his peculiar turns of phrase we have tried to give a direct translation. We strongly recommend to the reader the work of René Le Forestier on the Élus Coëns for greater insight into what Pasqually likely meant by some of his more enigmatic passages and phraseology.

We have corrected a few obvious printing errors. There are some dates, though, which while certainly printing errors, have been left as they appear in the text. Therefore, certain dates should probably be checked against other sources. Quotation marks are used somewhat inconsistently throughout the text. Thus, it is sometimes unclear when Papus is writing himself and when he is quoting the correspondence. Context makes it evident in almost every case, but it is at times a little off-putting. We have, nevertheless, left the quotes and other conventions as they appear in the original text of Papus.

Just as we noted above that Papus tends to use his own peculiar terminology for the various Masonic Rites, he also often indiscriminately confuses the Élus Coëns, the Strict Observance, and the followers of Saint-Martin into one collective "Martinism." He is certainly not the first to do this, but even with the extensive resources he had at hand, he does nothing to dispel this notion. This may be in part in order to help further the aims of his own "Martinist" movement, which sought to synthesize the aforesaid movements, along with other strains of contemporary occultism. The strict researcher of Masonic history will see this as misleading and even deceptive, or at the very least sloppy scholarship. But we must also understand that Papus was an esotericist first, not an academic. That is, while the Masonic historian is looking at the history of the various rites and orders, the occultist is looking at the transmission of a *tradition* that remains largely distinct from the vehicles through which it passes. This crucial point is utterly overlooked and incomprehensible to the profane (uninitiated) scholars. This is why Papus is so beloved by fellow mystics while being scorned and scoffed at by the academics. It is likely not the case that Papus was unaware of the external reality of the various temporal movements. It is just that he saw them as of secondary importance to the secret inner tradition that has passed through so many religions, philosophical schools, and fraternities. And it is this essential tradition that had come to Papus and that he coalesced in his Ordre Martiniste, in particular in the grade of Superieur Inconnu, or Unknown Superior, which, of course, is the only true grade of Martinist initiation.

This work is not perfect, but it is not nearly as flawed as some would have us believe. To the researcher and esotericist alike, this brief study gives a wealth of information drawn directly from primary source materials. Of particular interest are the catechisms included in the Appendix. Not all of the catechisms of the Order are included here; and there are a few mistakes, such as some likely transcription errors, as well as what appears to be a few missing lines from a couple of the catechisms. Still, what is here comprises the bulk of the catechetical materials and offers a penetrating look into the fascinating and unique doctrine of the Élus Coëns as Masonic Rite and occult theurgical school. Additionally, Papus' commentary gives sometimes unexpected insight into the historical context, and even dispels a few falsehoods often perpetuated concerning his own Martinist school. For instance, it has been claimed by some Martinist obediences that the concept of Initiateurs Libres, or Free Initiators, was a relatively late, post-Papus, invention, and that in the era of Papus and Chaboseau the S.I. was the ultimate empowerment, or that an initiator's powers were only tied to a Lodge or Supreme Council. But Papus, writing here in 1895, puts that notion unquestionably to rest: "Moreover, a great number of Free Initiators S.·. I.·. assure in a definitive manner the propagation of the Order." This concept reflects a core initiatic tenet, which is that an Order is only created to serve as vehicle for the initiation. The initiation, if it is authentic, does not *issue from* the Order, it merely *passes through* the Order. Papus understood this well, as did Pasqually before him, which is why Pasqually's ostensibly Masonic rite was only incidentally or "accidentally" (to use the language of the church) Masonic, not substantially so. The Masonic Rite of the Élus Coëns, as all esoteric Masonic Rites, was merely a convenient framework by which the "cult of the divinity" could be practiced.

Sâr Phosphoros
Sovereign Grand Commander
Christian Knights of Saint-Martin

INTRODUCTION

Up to the present, we have not possessed any serious documents permitting the elucidation of the life of one of the men who have most contributed to the development and propaganda of illuminism in France, Martinès de Pasqually, the initiator of Claude de Saint-Martin called the Philosophe Inconnu [Unknown Philosopher], and the founder of the Rite of Élus Coëns.

Representative of the Martinist tradition, we have been placed in a position, thanks to our Lodge of Lyon, to study some archives miraculously saved and which cast a decisive light upon the history of illuminism in France in the 18th century, and upon the relationship of the Lodges with the Strict Observance of the Baron de Hundt.

These archives originate with a man scarcely known by the special authors, J.-B. Willermoz, placed at the head of the esoteric movement at Lyon, and who has enjoyed one of the most important roles in the history of Martinism.

Among the precious documents that these archives contain, we have especially studied:

1. The correspondence of Martinès de Pasqually with Willermoz (1767-1774).
2. The correspondence of Louis-Claude de Saint-Martin with Willermoz, *correspondence from initiate to initiate*, comprised of forty-eight letters (1771-1790).
3. The correspondence of some other initiates such as the abbé Fournier (ten letters, 1778-1787), plus the catechisms, the written communications, and the rituals of the Élus Coëns and the Chevaliers Bienfaisants de la Cité Sainte [Knights Beneficent of the Holy City].

One understands how much attention this classification requires in order to be done carefully, and in order to finally allow the establishment of a true history of illuminism in France.

Therefore, we have decided to divide the work into three parts, each forming a work distinct from the rest. We will therefore dedicate a special study,

1st, to Martinès de Pasqually;

2nd, to Louis-Claude de Saint-Martin;

3rd, to Willermoz and to his documents arising in great part from the Convent of Wilhemsbad.

It is the study dedicated to Martinès de Pasqually that we deliver today to the public. This work was begun by us at Lyon, on location, last July (1893) and pursued until this day (October 16) without interruption.

In order to indicate to the readers, the character of our research, we are going to approach successively the following points:

1. State of the letters of Martinès de Pasqually (orthographic style, matters treated).
2. Research concerning the authenticity of these documents; history of the archives.
3. Method that we have followed for the publication of these documents; life, work of Martinès; personal clarifications.
4. Refutation of the inevitable errors committed by the historians, fault of certain documents.

The letters from Martinès to Willermoz, deduction made from the accessory sheets and from the copies are numbered at twenty-eight thus arranged:

2 letters in-folio of 4 pages,	June 19, 1767, September 19, 1767
1 letter in-folio of 4 pages,	June 20, 1768
6 letters in-folio of 4 pages,	September 2, 1768
-- in-folio - 3 -	- September 11, 1768
-- in-4to - 3 -	- September 18, 1768
-- in-4to - 3 -	- September 27, 1768
-- -- - 4 -	- October 2, 1768

-- -- - 3 -	- September 25, 1768
5 letters in-folio of 4 pages,	- January 23, 1769
-- in-4to - 4 -	- February 19, 1769
-- -- - 5 -	- May 3, 1769
-- -- - 4 -	- April 8, 1769
-- -- - 3 -	- August 29, 1769
6 letters in-folio of 4 pages,	- January 20, 1770
-- in-4to - 4 -	- February 16, 1770
-- in-folio - 4 -	- March 13, 1770
-- in-4to - 4 -	- April 7, 1770
-- -- - 8 -	- July 11, 1770
-- -- - 3 -	- December 16, 1770
3 letters in-4to of 3 pages,	- August 27, 1771
-- -- - 3 -	- November 1, 1771
-- -- - 3 -	- November 26, 1771
2 letters in-4to of 2 pages,	- January 13, 1772
-- -- - 2 -	- April 17, 1772
1 letters in-4to of 4 pages,	- October 12, 1773
2 letters in-4to of 3 pages,	- April 24, 1774
-- -- - 4 -	- August 3, 1774

All these letters are perfectly preserved.

The style of these letters is relatively clear when one considers that they have been written by a foreigner. The ideas set forth are most often very elevated, principally each time that the master touches on the doctrine.

The orthography is sometimes rather bizarre, and we have had to make true translations from the extracts that we cite in the course of this work; this was one of the most arduous parts of our task. Without this precaution it would be impossible for the reader to follow the thoughts of Martinès. We give as an example the following simple extract according to the letter of September 19, 1767.

"Delay must be attributed to a rather considerable illness which held me nearly a month and a half, now in a position to be able to support my head on my shoulders on account of a frightful inflammation that I had at the end of my right ear, I had furthermore a more considerable flu, all falling upon my chest, joined with all its evils a stitch and a good fever. I ask myself if only one of all its evils would not be enough for me to repent for some fault that I may have committed against the Grand Master, supposing that I had not perceived it myself."

As we shall see by the following, each letter enters upon the most diverse subjects while insisting particularly on various points: the initiation of Willermoz into the practice, and the constitution of the society of Willermoz.

All the authors who have spoken of the founder of Martinism wrote his name: *Martinez de Pasqualis*.

But all the letters addressed to Willermoz are signed:

Don Martinès de Pasqually

One letter of November 1, 1771 is signed:

Depasqually de la Tour

And it is to this name that Martinès had his correspondence sent at Paris:

"*Depasqually de la Tour, at the Trois-Rois, Montorgueil street, near the Cómedie italienne.*" (Letter from Paris from April 27, 1771.)

Also, the letters written rapidly are signed:

D.P.D.L.T.

Abbreviation of the preceding signature. (Letter from Bordeaux from November 26, 1771.)

However, the official acts are generally signed as Don Martinès de Pasqually, Grand Sovereign, and this signature is followed by the esoteric seal of Martinès. This seal rather often replaces the signature. (Letter from Port-au-Prince from April 24, 1774.)

Finally, in a letter from April 17, 1772 announcing the initiation of Saint-Martin, the seal and another sign which accompanies it are marked twice.

∴

What deduction may we draw from this signature?

We will insist presently only upon one sole point.

Note the word Don, written with an N and not with an M. We may admit that whatever contempt Martinès had had for orthography, he at least knew how to write his name correctly. Now, a Portuguese would have qualms about always writing DOM before his name, and those who know the local prejudices know that he would never be anxious to be confused with a Spaniard in writing DON.

Until there is proof of the contrary, we will persist then to not consider Martinès as Portuguese.

This leads us to verify the character of authenticity of the letters of the master.

The documents that we possess have indeed the most complete character of authenticity. But he is always found of gloomy spirits to which the historical and moral proofs are not equal, and which require one of these proofs by the fact, irrefutable in their brutality. Without dwelling on the concordance of dates, the exactitude of the details evoked, notably in what concerns Saint Martin, we did our best to discover an official document corroborating the indications contained in the letters that we possess. To this effect, two acts were of the greatest importance to us. First of all, the record of marriage of Martinès, which would have indicated to us the exact age and true homeland of the master; then the record of birth of his son. We wrote to Bordeaux, and we must render homage publicly to the courtesy with which Mr. Duval, archivist of the town, was willing to place himself entirely at our disposal. We had first asked Mr. Duval to have some searches carried out concerning the marriage record. Here is the letter that he sent to us on this subject:

Bordeaux, 4 July, 1893.

Sir,

Conforming to your request, I have done some research concerning the marriage record of Martinès de Pasquallis, staying at Bordeaux from September 2-10, 1767, according to your notes.

The lists for all the parishes of the town of the documents for the Catholics, Protestants, and Israelites have been perused from 1750 to 1780 and have not furnished any information, either in the name of Martinès or of Pasquallis.

Please accept, Sir, the assurance of my distinguished consideration.

Duval
Archivist of the town.

My efforts, for their part, seemed then to have to remain unfruitful. But Martinès announces in one of his letters the birth and baptism of his son. We returned then to the charge, furnishing to Mr. Duval as many notes as possible, and on July 21, we received the following letter, which confirms in an absolute manner the authenticity of the documents that we possess.

Bordeaux, July 31, 1893.

Sir,

I have seen to resuming the research relative to the marriage record of don Martinès de Pasquallis; they have not yielded any better results than those at the time of your first letter. It is therefore nearly certain that this marriage did not take place in Bordeaux.

I have been more successful with the baptismal record that you requested, and of which I send you hereafter the exact copy, in respecting the orthography thereof.

Please accept, Sir, the assurance of my perfect consideration.

Duval
Archivist of the Town

"In 1768, on June 20, has been baptized: master Jean Jaques Philipe Joachin Anselme de la Tour de la Case, legitimate son of sire Jaques Delivon Joachin Latour de la Case don Martinèts de Pasqually and lady Marguerite Angelique de Colas, de St. Michel; Godfather: François Vissières; godmother: Catherine Roussillon. The father has signed,

"*Signed the register*: don Martinès Depasqually, father; Arnaud Caprain; Canihac; Leris, vicar.

"In the margin is written: Baptism of master Jean Jaques Philipe Joachim Anselme de Pasqually."

(Municipal archives of Bordeaux, series GG, parochial registers, no. 240, parish of St. Croix, article 980.)

THE ARCHIVES

Now that we are assured of the real value of the letters of Martinès, let us summarize as best we can the history of the archives from Willermoz to the present day.

After the Convent of Wilhemsbadt where Martinism had played so important a role, an alliance had been concluded between the Martinists and the representatives of the Strict Observance. The archives destined to the creation of the Reformed Rite had been confided to the director of the Province of Auvergne, the V.P. Master, J.-B. Willermoz, merchant of Lyon. This occurred towards 1782. The negotiations were pursued during the following years, and in 1789 the introduction of the Revolution abruptly stopped the work in progress.

Let us leave the words to Willermoz in a letter written in 1810 to the Prince de Hesse:

"I was unaware of what had occurred in the various regions of France; for it was no longer possible to correspond at all. But two or three days before the beginning of the siege which threatened the town of Lyon, alarmed at the danger of letting slip away the provincial archives, the deposit of which was confided to me into the house of the Order, situated outside of town, I traveled there as secretly as possible with only one courageous armed guard. I emptied the cupboards; I piled up in haste what they contained into the trunks, and I was rather happy to see it enter into the town the same day; for, from the next day there was no more time, the bridge of communication from the town to the house of the Order having been broken; and three days later this house and all that I had not been able to remove was burned and reduced to ashes. A bomb fell on the house, in town where I had just taken asylum, reducing to dust one of these trunks filled with registers, minutes, and documents of every kind. After the siege, I saw myself obliged, by new, more pressing dangers which forced me to flee and hide, to reduce these archives to the smallest volume possible, in order to be able to carry with me what I had not been able to bury or to deposit in sure hands. I have been stopped and imprisoned three times and on the third, the very day when I was condemned to death for the next day, the fall of the atrocious tyrant of France, Robespierre, granted me liberty."

(Lett. to Prince de Hesse, p. 7 of the mss.)

This constant preoccupation with saving the archives in the midst of the most pressing dangers is admirable; and does it not merit the ardent recognition of all the sincere friends of Truth?

Some years later, Willermoz died and bequeathed the precious deposit to his nephew, whom he had initiated himself and named G.M. Profés. At the death of the latter, his wife confided the papers to a good friend, profoundly devoted to these ideas, Mr. Cavarnier.

In the midst of material success and daily labors, this right-thinking man found the time to pursue his studies and was led progressively to thoroughly investigate the occultism of which he had become a fervent adept, working alone and without confiding his research to any society.

But feeling the heaviness of the responsibility that weighed upon him, should the archives be lost, Cavarnier had, without a second doubt, the intense desire to save the sacred deposit, and we know all the power with which the desire propagates in the invisible.

One day, passing before a small bookshop, Cavarnier is drawn, despite himself, toward this store. He enters, chats with the person that he finds there, and states (perhaps without astonishment, for the intuitives are subject to this sort of thing), that he has found before him the representative of Martinism at Lyon, Mr. Elie Steel, and that he has been led to the direct successors of those whose archives he possesses.

What to say after that. Notified of what occurred, our friend Vitte did not hesitate to send word to me at Lyon where, for a week, I inspected and copied the principal documents. I had the pleasure to go to Cavarnier, and I found in him a great-hearted man, worthily chosen by our masters to be the guardian of their spirituality.

It is in this way that I have been able to reconstitute a great part of this book and of the work of Martinès, and that I have succeeded in clarifying certain points on the Life of Saint-Martin, obscure for his best biographer, Mr. Matter.

In all this my merit is naught; for I am not but a humble instrument chosen by our masters to bring to the light of day what they have saved across so many vicissitudes. My sole ambition is to be a faithful commentator and an enlightened interpreter of the documents whose publication they have wished to confide in me.

If, however, my efforts betray my goodwill, I will at least do my best so that another may be more fortunate than me in furnishing to my readers the majority of the originals in all their integrity. I hope thus to respond as best I can to the great favor of which I have had the honor to be the object. This will be my sole recompense as it is my sole ambition.

∴

In order to justify the aim, what method of publication must be adopted?

Must the letters of Martinès be published without commentary? This would leave to the care of the reader a meticulous work requiring too much time. Furthermore, if the character of Saint-Martin lends itself more to such a method of publication, the multiplicity of subjects touched on by Martinès in his letters renders such a means impossible to realize practically.

This is why we have analyzed each letter from a triple point of view.

1. From the point of view of material life, of the affairs and travels of Martinès.
2. From the point of view of the doctrine of the master and of his practical magic.
3. From the point of view of the practical realization and of the Society of the Élus Coëns.

Such is the raison d'être of each of the three chapters of this work.

Furthermore, we have seen to precede each of these divisions by a sort of preface summarizing our personal ideas touching on the Martinist doctrine (chap. 2) and the character of the secret societies according to the teachings of esotericism.

We do not speak on the work that has required of us an elucidation on the practical magic of the founder of Martinism, no more than the research that demands a study of the situation of

Martinism in the bosom of the secret societies of this era. Those of our readers who do us the great honor of following our works are in a position to do us justice in this regard. As to our adversaries who see in our works only more or less pleasant compilations and who decorate us with the title of "vulgarizer of occultism," we do not seek to convince them, and we hope simply that they will value this work enough to pillage it on occasion... without citation of source according to their laudable custom.

The unexpected rewards that the invisible wastes on us, and the calm of a conscience certain to have done its duty, are blessings that no perfidy may await, and constitute the true source of happiness for incarnate man.

Those initiated into the high doctrine of Martinism understand us when we recall to them that their first duty is to remain *unknown* to those that we save from ignorance or egotism, and *superior* to all the injustices and all the villainies of the profane world.

Papus

FIRST CHAPTER

LIFE OF MARTINÈS DE PASQUALLY
(from 1767 to 1772)

Life of Martinès de Pasqually

Martinès arrived at Bordeaux towards the month of May, 1767, coming from Paris, and after having passed through Amboise, Blois, Tours, Poitiers, La Rochelle, Rochefort, Saintes, and Blayes.

In each of these towns he had put himself in touch with the Masons in order to combat the influence of the Lodge called Clermont, and in order to establish the foundations of an understanding with the Sovereign Tribunal of his Order of Élus Coëns. We will return to all these details concerning the work of realization of Martinès. For the moment, let us retain the itinerary of this journey which allows us to follow the "Grand Sovereign" in his mission of propaganda.

The letter of June 19, 1767, which gives us all these details, is dedicated purely to questions of the Order and is especially interesting in that it marks the beginning of the correspondence between Martinès and Willermoz, especially the initiatic correspondence.

The correspondence ceases abruptly at this moment only to resume three months later and, this time, we begin to understand some interesting details on our author (September 19, 1767).

Several important events had been produced since the arrival of Martinès at Bordeaux.

First of all, a rather serious illness which had lasted a month and a half and whose description deserves to be carefully reported.

Illness of Martinès

"A rather considerable illness which has kept me for nearly a month and a half from being able to support my head on my shoulders on account of a frightful inflammation that I had in the corner of my right ear; I had, moreover, a considerable flu. It all fell upon my chest; add to all these ailments a stitch in my side and a strong fever. I ask you if any one of these ailments were not enough to repent for some fault that I may have committed against the Grand Master, supposing that I had not noticed it."

This takes us from June 19 to around the middle of August, especially if one realizes that this illness, probably the consequence of the fatigue of travel, must have broken only some days after the sending of the letter of June. Scarcely recovered, what did Martinès do?

He got married.

Marriage of Martinès

This question of the marriage of Pasqually is very important, for it is still ignored by all those who have had to concern themselves with the master. It throws, furthermore, a great light on the origin of the relations that would be established later between Martinès and Saint-Martin.

"I do not count on being able to return to Paris to my Sovereign Tribunal, as they have made me promise for the rest of this month, because of my lack of health as well as my particular affairs and those of the house of the young lady that I have wedded, fifteen days ago, in this land, who is the niece of the old major of the regiment of Foix."

The marriage has therefore had to have taken place at the beginning of September, 1767, and it is through his wife that

Martinès is put in touch with the officers of this regiment of Foix from where arose his most illustrious adepts.

THE WIFE OF PASQUALLY

It is interesting to note some details on the woman that the master had just wed.

We know that this young lady is the niece of the old major of the regiment of Foix.

The correspondence of Willermoz contains two letters from Madame Pasqually.

The one that is most useful to us for the moment is from May 4, 1771, and concerns the request of a gown. It is signed,

COLAS DE PASQUALLY

It may be read Colar, but Willermoz has taken care to well establish the orthography of the name in the annotation placed on the back of the letter.

We have therefore conducted some research bearing on this name of Colas.

First of all, we have studied in the military profession of France "the history of the Regiment of Foix."

In the Register of 1761, we find Mr. the Comte de Rouge, colonel since 1758; Mr. de Lefrat, lieutenant-colonel, and Mr. Collas, major.

Until 1762 we find the name of Mr. Collas as major. "The Register" of 1763 informs us that by decree of December 10, 1762, "the regiment of Foix is destined to the service of the Navy and the Colonies, and to guard the ports of the Kingdom." That is why we no longer find the name of the Colonel: the Comte de Maulevrier-Langeron at *San Domingo.*

It is more than likely at this period that Mr. Collas, major of the regiment and uncle of Madame de Pasqually, has retired from military life.

THE SON OF MARTINÈS

The letter of June 20, 1768, gives us some very curious and very instructive information. We see that Martinès dedicates all his intellectual forces to the propagation of his doctrines and his order, that he begins to notice the hostility of one of its members, the Master du Guers, who will soon be driven from the society, and finally that he is prepared to constitute a new Sovereign Tribunal locale. We will rediscover the names of the members composing this tribunal with respect to the lodges.

But a great event had occurred unexpectedly in the private life of the master: he has just had a son whom he has received as Grand Master after having him baptized. We find here the first proof of the falsity of the allegations of those who claim that Martinès is Jewish; we will have later on another stronger one if it is possible. But let us cite the original phrase.

"I announce to you V.P. Master that the son that God has given me has been received Grand Master Coëns last Sunday after his baptism at the 7th hour of the last solar horizon, conforming to our laws, assisted by four of my old simple Coëns named above."

It is in this letter that we find for the first time the seal of the Grand Sovereign and the esoteric signature, the secret seal of Martinès.

We also point out the description of a "vision" that the master has had on the subject of the sister of Willermoz struck by a uterine ailment and a list of medical prescriptions to fulfill. Martinès reveals himself to us as a physician.

What, then, is his school from the point of view of the medical theories?

MARTINÈS HEALER

His opinions derive from a curious mixture between the "humorist" theories in vogue at the time and the medicine of the countryside. We shall see.

First the pathology:

"Here is her illness, which I told you gives you no trouble. Her sickness is an overflow of spermatic liquids that are reintegrated, after its insensible expulsion, into the conception bed, and there is subdivided into all the matriculary branches, which gives great and even unsustainable pains to the person that they affect, by the great tension which is made in all the membranes and branches which contain it in its equilibrium. It ought even to be descended therefore towards her orifice and it is then that this womb, when your sister makes some slightly strong movement, ought to feel rather strong pains as if something tore her kidneys, along the thighs and the top of the knees, in a word, my V.P. Master, I have nothing more to tell you in the detail of this sickness except that the womb to the intestinal parts of a woman is and does the same things that does the lung to the chest. If the lung is enflamed, the cartilaginous parts of the chest suffer, likewise the walls of the womb suffer by the lack of humectation which causes an inflammation as much to it as to its surroundings."

This pathology where one senses some anatomical knowledge mixed with a curious intuition of the homological connections (uterus and chest) is moreover curious by the search for causes.

But let us touch on the therapeutics:

"For this effect, according to the divine precept: help yourself, I will help you, the remedy must be carried to the disease. You will take the four milks that we call the four succors, which are cow's milk, goat's milk, ass's milk, and sheep's milk, about half a cup of each in which you dissolve a quarter ounce of pure spermaceti. Put all of it into a bottle of white glass and no other. You heat it all for a good quarter of an hour in the double boiler which will be in a new pot of spring water; you attach there the aforesaid bottle where will be the spermaceti and the different milks, so that the bottle does not touch the pot in any manner, and that it be well suspended in the air in the water. The whole thing is placed cold, the bottle is left open, and when the water is quite hot, at the aforesaid time, you withdraw all outside of the fire, you let it lose a great heat all together, then you take the bottle of milk from the pot, and when it is tepid, you put it in a small syringe that you give to the sick in order to syringe the womb...She will take these small anodynes, as much as she judges fitting, she may take two in the morning, two in the afternoon, and even one in the evening and even more if she feels, which does not cause any pain to use this remedy. Tell her that I assure her of a perfect success."

Thus, here is one of the most important letters since we see Martinès in a light little known unto the present. But let us move on.

OCCUPATION OF M. AT BORDEAUX

The Master was occupied at Bordeaux with three orders of works.

1. The making of the initiation papers.
2. The propagation of his Order and the foundation of new lodges, as well as the development of his lodge at Bordeaux.

3. The works of practical magic and the teaching of practical magic to some chosen disciples.

There are, certainly, what fills the moments left free, the occupations destined to assure material life.

Thus, as soon as a disciple may make the trip, he hastens to rush to Bordeaux in order to work with the master.

The letter of August 13, 1768, tells us of the arrival of master du Guers, as we will soon discover. Furthermore, it contains the first initiatic teachings with which we will occupy ourselves in another chapter; finally, it announces the first relations with St. Martin, still a profane.

"I inform you that Mr. de Saint-Martin wrote me that he is to come to pass his winter quarter here, perhaps with the V.P. Master de Grainville. I likewise await the V.P. Master de Balzac who is to come down from Rochelle to come here to stay some days with me for their instruction and in order to receive their constitutive patents to raise temples in the lands where they will come to stay at the end of September or the beginning of October."

Some notes on these personalities.

Saint-Martin, who will later be the most ardent and most celebrated of the disciples of Martinès, is yet a profane, therefore they call him Mister.

De Grainville, who will be the colleague of Saint-Martin in his initiatic career, is at this moment captain of the Regiment of Foix if we refer ourselves to "the military Register of France" from 1767 and 1768.

De Balzac is a member of the branch of the Balzacs of La Rochelle, and despite all my research, it has been impossible for me to establish any familial link whatsoever between the initiate of Martinès and the great writer, who has remained ennobled himself: Honoré de Balzac. The research was all the more tempting since Honoré de Balzac had surely known the Martinist doctrines; but by what path? Mystery.

Martinès therefore works much, as much practice as theory. This is what the letter of September 2, 1768 teaches us.

This letter, written to respond to certain requests of Willermoz concerning the practice, teaches us at the same time that Martinès, aided by du Guers, is working on the construction of rituals.

"I am so pressed, just as the P. Master Du Guers, to finish all our degrees, as well as all the ceremonies and catechisms in order to send them to Paris, so that the Sovereign Tribunal may be filled with all the objects that it calls for (requests) in order to satisfy its grand temples, its lodges, as well as all its members, on which I will not say much."

Willermoz, however, was not deprived, for on September 11, 1768, Martinès sent him an enormous letter of 4 pages in-folio, uniquely dedicated to the magical practices and that we will reproduce in extenso in one of the following chapters.

For the moment, we will simply study the life of Martinès and his daily works at Bordeaux.

Therefore, we will leave for now the letters of September 18, 1768, of September 27, 1768, and of October 2, 1768, which have connection with the magical operations and with a misunderstanding which had prevented Willermoz from receiving the packages in time because of the carelessness of a domestic servant.

We will retain from these letters only this last detail which shows that Martinès lived modestly; but was able, nevertheless, to have a service and even to receive several friends to stay with him as we will see hereafter.

The letter of October 2 also announces to us the arrival of his awaited friends at Bordeaux.

"I inform you of the arrival of de Grainville in Bordeaux with Master de Saint-Martin who comes for personal affairs. Master de Grainville lodges and eats with me. I am waiting at this time the

Master de Balzac who is at La Rochelle. I expect that he has just embarked for Bordeaux."

Finally, this letter ends by new medical counsels on the sister of his correspondent.

DU GUERS AFFAIR

On November 25, 1768, is written a letter relating to the betrayal of the master du Guers.

The conduct of this individual is, indeed, singular. After having received the direct teachings of Martinès, he pursues only a sole aim: to make money. He therefore sells degrees to the highest offer; he gives Masonic initiations for more or less elevated sums; finally, he betrays at once his masters and his oaths.

Here is what Martinès first said of it.

"And in order to avoid having him make use of my name and my instructions, I have removed him entirely from among me and have left him to the mercy of the Great Architect of the Universe; it is necessary to pray him that he have mercy on him; but he has rendered himself unworthy of the confidence of men."

According to what Martinès says, this du Guers passed himself off as the sole Grand Master of the Order, taking the lead over the entire direction from Paris.

This letter also informs us that Saint-Martin has received the first degrees; for he is already Venerable Master.

"You may write to P.Mtr. de Grainville who gives you very kind regards as well as the Vble. Mtr. de Saint-Martin; they are waiting to hear from you..."

The Du Guers scandal continued for a long time, for on January 23, 1769, a long letter gives us some very interesting details on the various phases of this affair.

Du Guers, by his true name Bonnichon, is definitively stricken from the Order; but he went to everyone to destroy Martinès and his society. Judge for yourself:

"The operations" had, it appears, manifested by obvious signs the unworthiness of Du Guers who has withdrawn outside a session "covered with shame and confusion."

"This monster has conspired with several disreputable persons, and other persons that I had formerly driven from my old temple in order to astonish the good faith of the magistrates and their justice by false accusations that he brings to them against me, in telling them that I was nothing but a foreigner and adventurer in Bordeaux, that I have dishonored him in all the good houses of the town where I have protected him.

"Having been warned of the proceedings of this rogue, I found the Arch Jurat, gentleman before whom he had presented his complaint and his impostures. Seeing me, he was rather surprised, having the honor of being particularly known to him, and asked me for some information on the account of this man. Upon which I instructed him by finishing my instruction on this subject that the aforesaid du Guers was a swindler under the pretext of Masonry and put the proof in his hands; I even added all the vileness, the baseness, and impiety that this imposter has shown here at Bordeaux for more than four months.

"I have told enough of this to the magistrates so that they sent for him and scolded him cruelly in causing him serious prohibitions and forbidding him in the future from making any more complaints unless he would have business with them. And they sent him away again covered in rags and humiliation.

"He wished to certify to the magistrates that he was a man of great consequence and that he could prove it even by Messrs.

D'Aubenton and M. Caunaud, commissioner of the classes of our navy who would give him a certificate of all that he advanced before their justice. He was taken at his word. The magistrates immediately sent a city official to these gentlemen in order to request a certificate as the aforesaid chevalier had assured him; he was formally refused in saying that they only had the honor of knowing him through the recommendation that Mr. Dom Martinès had made. There was enough brought back to the judges for them to place this man lower than earth. I, charitably, not wishing to take advantage over the rights that I have to ruin this wretch, would be content myself to scorn him and abandon him to his unfortunate fate.

"But seeing that this man persisted in taking measures to try to harm me, saying everywhere that he would have me ruined before long, and that since the 'jurats' had not rendered any justice, he would bring his complaint to the attorney general and to the Marshals of France. In truth I was unable to prevent myself from revealing to the magistrates my swindler and errant knight. I detailed to Mr. d'Arche, jurat, the motives which had engaged this man to act so atrociously, against me, the Order, and its principal chiefs. Upon my exposé Mr. d'Arche sent for him AND ANNOUNCED TO HIM THAT HE HAD REFERRED HIM TO BE JUDGED BEFORE OUR SECRET TRIBUNAL[1] and that being accused of sharp prevarications in the Order, it was not proper to make a conflict of jurisdiction; just as he had done in bringing to several courts vague complaints against me and that consequently there would be present a trustworthy man from the town hotel who would be present and who rendered to them a faithful account of the judgment and decision against him.

"What was said was done; we instituted proceedings against him and he was given judgment by the secret tribunal on January 5, 1769, as you will see later on, seeing that I had some extracts drawn therefrom which I will send you before long. The next morning I myself brought the decision to Mr. d'Arches to whom I made the reading which he found good and deserving of the prevarications of this iniquitous man. From there I sent it to M. d'Aubenton who read it carefully and likewise found it good.

"I returned from there and made known his judgment to all persons, Masons and profanes, as well as to those to whom he had spoken ill of the Order and its head, which astonished them much.

"Finally, this man seeing himself definitively discovered, he was with his clique with the curé of my parish to tell him that I taught, under the pretext of Masonry, a sect contrary to the Christian religion. Having caught wind of this, I delivered myself to my curé and asked him what had been said to him on the part of this rogue against me. He made no mystery of it, he told me everything.

And I made him see that I was in my religion, my certificates of Catholicity[2] and my exact and essential duties of a zealous Christian, and he was convinced of the truth that I told him, just as the false exposé of this monster.

"When he was entirely informed by the one and the other, this swindler impostor, seeing that he could not succeed in his crimes, he decided to come to me one day when I was in the countryside with Mr. de Brulle, a King's guard, our emulator, in order to try to make the P.Mtrs. de Grainville and de Balzac feel the pain that he felt he had lost their friendship and esteem, and he would have me where he could kill me with a pistol shot. My guardian angel followed him then in order to piss in the bassinet. The P.Mtrs. brought something up to him on some subject, it matters not what, this ended it.

"This iniquitous man had affiliated to bastard and apocryphal lodges."

After several attempts to ruin the master, this du Guers received the order from the magistrates to embark in 24 hours, and he decided then to depart for Cayenne.

We now find a series of letters dated respectively from February 19, May 5, August 8, April 29, 1769, and from January 20, 1770, which contain above all information on the organization of the Order and which show that Martinès was actively occupied with the propaganda all while being rather difficult on the choice of the new members.

The second part of the letter of February 19 is from the hand of de Grainville and signed by him and makes reference to a request of funds by Martinès.

The letter of August 8 gives us some information on the affairs of Martinès, all the more precious since they are very rare in the correspondence.

"I would be quite resolved to stay at Paris just as they desire, but my present situation, my domestic affairs, and the recovery of a small inheritance that I have here from one of my deceased relatives in the islands, as I have made G. Master de la Chevalerie see, will keep me yet some time in this town."

We will see later that this inheritance will be the predominate cause of the departure of Martinès for San Domingo.

With these letters are found joined a response from Willermoz and it must be acknowledged that the disciple is not very affectionate towards his master. He responds to the request for payment made by de Grainville on February 18.

He has expected to be at Paris in order to do it, so that his letter is dated from April 29, 1769.

Seeing the importance of this letter, we believe it necessary to reproduce it *in-extenso*, for it sets a critical period of the history of Martinèsism.

TO DOM MARTINÈS

"Paris, this April 29, 1769.

"Dear V.P. and V.R.S.

"I have received in plenty of time at Lyon your last letter of February 19 added to that of P.M. de Grainville by which you wrote me to not do any work for the equinox of March, and the reasons that you had them suspended even for yourself; as this is beyond my comprehension I do not enter into any detail on the above, and I have conformed myself to your intentions.

"The P.M. de Grainville informed me on his part of the necessity that there would be for the good of the Order for you to return to Paris in order to put all the degrees in order there under the eyes of the P.M. de la Chevalerie and de Lusignan, of your difficulty with the acquittal of the debts that you have contracted at Bordeaux, and of the necessity of making arrangements for the Order to provide for you in the future.

"I have guessed at the true foundations of the P.M.'s reason, but as I have not received any clarification on the above from the P.M. residing in Paris, I have postponed responding to you on this subject until returning myself to Paris that I might confer with them, which I have done immediately upon my arrival into this town; I have found the P.M. de la Chevalerie and de Lusignan very little disposed to do what the M. de Grainville asks in your name, and displeased with the excess of your proceedings towards them and towards the Order. To get to the point, they have communicated to me all the correspondence held between the Orients of Bordeaux and Paris since my trip last year, I admit to you frankly P.M. that one may not read it with composure, it seems that you have sought every possible means to humiliate the P.M. substitute that you yourself have specially charged with the affairs of the Order; even if you would have no other means to know the men but those which are general to the human species, you could not place the conduct and sentiments of the P.M. substitute only equal with that of Mr. Duguers. The one enjoys the most positive and well-deserved reputation, and the other already earned your resentment by a great number of excesses to which he was prone and of which you were instructed either by the M. substitute or by me. Nevertheless, as soon as he appeared at Bordeaux you received him with the greatest confidence though well warned of his bad conduct and all the wrongs have been towards M. substitute, there is nothing more humiliating and disgusting for him; do not believe that it is my attachment to him that gives me bias or inspires in me the least partiality, it is on the reading of your own letters that I have judged you thus, and one may not judge otherwise; it was necessary for you to become the victim of Mr. Duguers in order to open your eyes in his regard, and I admit frankly that this has troubled me greatly. You have assured so often that your science gave you infallible means to know the heart of men, that seeing to what point you have been deceived on this occasion, I am reduced to doubt more strongly than ever a science that is too sublime so that an intelligent man may add there full and entire faith upon other witnesses than one's own, the assurance that you have given me often on the truth of la Chose, renewed then by the M. de Grainville, encouraged moreover by the M. substitute whom I have known for a long time, whose integrity has given me enough confidence to enter into the career, I have followed exactly and with good faith, all that has been prescribed to me without being any more successful, and I am still as disposed to follow it when I see dissipate the clouds that have gathered, not wishing by too much haste to lose the success that I have been promised, but once the confidence is destroyed, distaste follows. To say nothing, moreover, and your own letters tend to destroy it, that Mr. Duguers had to convince you to give the *things in truth*, these are the very words of your letter; we have not entered into the truth, we are therefore abused; judge for yourself where these reflections lead us and you create them; there are not two means in this matter to lead to the proposed aim. The truth is the only one, the goal of everything is unworthy of the honest man, if you judge me incapable of succeeding in the truth, tell me plainly, I will not complain at all and I will try to render myself worthy; in the perplexity that your letters throw us we must require of you some unequivocal proofs of the truth of la Chose which places us in a condition to judge for ourselves; show us sincerely the true way, prescribe the most exact means, without doubt this would be good and then the order will be engaged in showing you its rebirth and making set arrangements for the future, which Messrs. de la Chevalerie and de Lusignan have done in the past and tells you of their good will later. I will contribute willingly as much as my means will permit me since I will do what I hold myself; solid establishments will be formed and finally all will be disposed to make the arrangements that you desire; but at the present what can we do to sustain an edifice that you yourself announce to be built on sand. We have at Lyon 5 initiates, to whom I have promised instructions for more than a year without having received any. I have there a number of very suitable subjects, and already at the first sign, but I would hesitate to have made the least expenditure without being sure myself of the aim to which they aspire. The temple of Lyon may in very little time take on a real consistency; it is to you to throw up its foundations, you will find there your advantage and to us the satisfaction that we desire.

"Pardon, P.M., the frankness with which I write you on the state of things. It must be explained in good faith in order to settle the fate of each. I do not seek to offend you, but to be clear once and for all, I want to be able to announce to Lyon an object true and worthy of honest folks, and not to have there a charlatan; you will not fault, I think, my fastidiousness, the sentiments of M. de la Chevalerie and de Lusignan are the same, we are explained above; they are rebuffed by your proceedings. You can still repair all; your interests could not be placed in better hands. The Order demands the execution of your promises, nothing could be fairer.

"I am not able to make a long stay here, I have nevertheless the time to receive your response and to make one to you in my turn if your affairs permit you to do it soon. I would be pleased before leaving this town to see a definitive arrangement made and confidence restored.

"Glavot house, wig-maker, Golet-des-Bourdonnois street."

The response of Martinès is from August 8, and it is one of his most beautiful letters by the elevation of ideas. - We reproduce a large part of it in the chapter on Doctrine.

In another letter from January 20, 1770, Martinès returns to his financial difficulties:

"I assure you that if I had received some funds from the islands that I expect a considerable inheritance that I have had in these lands; I will not regret at all to go myself to install you and have you work vigorously."

On February 16, 1770, a new letter is sent nearly entirely dedicated to the details of magical ritual (4 p. in-folio). We draw from there nevertheless some useful information on the private life of the Master.

"I am no longer staying with Mr. Carvallo, old Jew, because of the assassination that he wished to commit against his cook, and for wanting to enjoy it. He is delivered to the justice that has been decreed; they pursued him vigorously at the tournelle. This is the third time that this has happened to him. This is a quite unfortunate Hebrew, perverted and not converted, that he renounced it in order to marry a Christian creature. My address is on the same street: Maison Poiraud, near the currency door.

"My wife is dangerously sick. She was brought imprudently to a considerable ruin outside the ability to be looked after by the faculty, except by me in the presence of a brother. She is still bedridden, but entirely if it pleases God, out of danger."

The letter of March 13, 1770, is entirely dedicated to magic and will be reproduced in-extenso in our chapter destined to this subject.

The letter of April 7, 1770, describes in detail the magical operation that has permitted the master to restore life to his dying wife. The end of this letter is dedicated to "La Chose."

THE DEBTS OF THE MASTER

We finally find, dated July 11, 1770, a response in 12 articles made by Martinès to the requests of the brethren of Paris. This important piece will be published in our chapter dedicated to the realization of the work of the master. We separate only the following passage which treats on the material affairs. (The analysis is in the hand of Willermoz.)

"The M.D.M. has not been able to respond sooner to the propositions because of the last illness of his mother-in-law which has caused him to suspend all correspondence.

"1. He thanks L.T.S. for his offers which prove the true zeal that the R+ have for la Chose; he owed around 3000£; he has paid the major part thereof, he remains owing still 1000£ which he hopes to pay by constraining himself yet some time. Then he will be free and able to leave Bordeaux without fearing any affront to his creditors to which he would be exposed if he left there before being entirely settled."

Thus, one year earlier, the brethren of Paris, suspicious of the teachings of Martinès, refused the payment requested by the intermediary of de Grainville. Now it is the master who gives them a lesson by refusing a pecuniary support that they had made him wait so long for. Moreover, it suffices to read this document in its entirety, in order to see the greatness of the sentiments invoked by Martinès to the support of his sincerity and good faith.

Saint-Martin understood so well the difficulties, to speak on these high questions to the ambitious, that he isolated himself and absolutely refused to associate himself with the existing Masonic lodges. But let us not take this up yet.

On December 16, Martinès wrote that he was returning to stay some days in the countryside. He was occupied "with pursuing vigorously some indispensible temporal affair," according to his expression. He had just, however, finished a "considerable work" which indicates that he had not wasted his time during this period from July to December. We learn further that "the master de Saint-Martin has been here for eight days in order to pursue his instructions and for the advantage of those of the R. +."

The rest of the letter is devoted to administrative questions.

Among the other documents we find a letter from Madame Colas de Pasqually, dated from May 4, 1771, and asking Willermoz to send a silk gown. This detail is interesting, for we are going to see later the pecuniary difficulties which fetter the realization of the work of Martinès, precisely in connection with the payment of this silk gown.

Here we are then at the year 1771. Martinès has made the trip to Paris. This journey promised since 1767 is finally executed, and the master stays at the following address: Maître de Pasqually de la Tour, at the 3 Rois, Montorgueil Street, near the Comédie italienne. This important letter of August 25, 1771, deserves a particular analysis. Let us reproduce first *in extenso* the beginning:

"I have received, my dear master and friend, your last letter, which master de Saint-Martin, my good friend, has sent me from Bordeaux. I am very grieved to be unable to respond to all it contains, as well as to assist you in your impending work; I counsel you to suspend it for the present moment, being forced, for some affairs of the utmost temporal importance, to remain all next September at Paris; in order to see finished with the ministers a project advantageous to the public, to the State, and to the most oppressed nation. All my statements are remitted to the public offices. I expect the success thereof as they have caused me to hope in it; if it takes place, as I think, it will be necessary for me to perhaps go to Lyon in order to confer with you, being unable to write you of this undertaking so as not to divulge the secret, being the soul of the affairs. It is an undertaking which is advantageous for the contractors and for the public. I count on you taking part in this affair as I have placed there some of your goof friends.

"I have found at my arrival in Paris, Mr. and Mrs. de L.[3] departed for their country home. I learn here that they have intended to come to take me to Bordeaux. I have written them to do what they can, to come to Paris towards the end of September. They will not be working here this time, any more than you."

Martinès speaks again of de Grainville and on the magical operations. He relates then in detail his conversations with the abbé Rozier and recommends him to Willermoz. Finally, we learn that the master is accompanied at Paris by Mtr. de la Boris.

"M. de la Boris, my second self that I have here with me, charges me to speak well to you of things on his part, as well as Mr. Caignet."

We come at the end to the question of the famous gown of Madame.

"As regards Madame's gown, send it at your liking, with the usual prices."

And, in the margin:

"Note for me the price of the gown and to whom I should send the money at Bordeaux."

On the back of the letter, we find this note in the hand of Willermoz:

"Brocaded taffeta 4/24-25 Na-P. 685 base white, striped stained rose 16½ to 13 £214.10. Remitted to M. Clairjon de Cramail at Lyon on September 20, 1771. - Remit the 214.10 above to M. Razurel, uncle and nephew, at Paris."

Thus, the gown of Madame de Pasqually cost 214 pounds 10, a relatively weak sum, that Martinès could not, however, succeed in paying.

While we are occupied with the material details, let us point out this note in the letter from Martinès:

"The young lady that I have found here in very bad health begins to do a little better. She charges me to tell you a thousand things on her part: she has not received any sausages."

Thus, is ended this curious and important document, which relates to the journey of the master to Paris.

This is only addressed from Paris. The correspondence resumes at Bordeaux on November 1, 1771.

"If I have delayed so long to respond to your requests and to the letter that you wrote me concerning the sending of the gown that you have been good enough to send to Madame, it is because I have been obliged to be on the roads and paths in several towns of our province, for my own domestic affairs. And besides, I have been obliged to accompany the chevalier d'Arc and the abbé de Langeac to la Réole, in order to take possession of the priory of la Réole, which this latter has taken. This last trip has kept me much longer than I wanted, which is the cause of me suspending all my correspondences.

"In regard to the amount of the gown that you told me by your letter to pay at Paris to your correspondent, I was no longer at Paris when you sent word of your desire. Your letter has reached me at Bordeaux.

"I was unable to refuse to accompany M. the chevalier d'Arc for the whole stay that he made in our province, in regard to all the goodness that he had for me during my stay at Paris. This is a gentleman of great credit of all civilities, being the first cousin once removed of our King.

"As regards the payment of the amount of Madame's gown, I would ask you if it is possible from now to the next fair of Bordeaux, being a little deprived of money for the arrangement of my temporal affairs."

Thus, there is that unfortunate question of the gown that reappeared. We will return to it again.

Let us also point out, in this letter, the following sentence, which comes after a new recommendation concerning magical practice:

"I inform you that I have finally obtained the cross of Saint-Louis from my Father-in-law."

Despite all our research into the special works, it has been impossible for us to retrieve the name of this father-in-law of whom Martinès speaks among the Chevaliers [Knights] of Saint-Louis.

This letter tells us further of the departure for Port-au-Prince of Cagne, commissioner general of the navy and cousin of Martinès.

"I instruct you further that I have delivered the constitutive patents to my cousin Cagnet."

Finally, let us not continue without indicating the post-scriptum:

"The master de Saint-Martin works ever for us."

As one may see, Saint-Martin takes a more and more active part in the theoretical and practical works of Martinès. This point will be even further brought to light later by the correspondence of the Master. Several letters are indeed in the writing of Saint-Martin, who lent his kind help in the capacity of secretary. This is particularly the case with the letter of January 13, 1772, of which we are now going to occupy ourselves.

This letter, very short (two pages in-8vo), contained only some information of an administrative order for the choice of members for the Lodge of Lyon and some counsel relative to the practice.

It is likewise in the letter of March 24, 1772, still in the writing of Saint-Martin, written following the failure of Willermoz in his experiments.

By contrast, the letter of April 17 and 30, 1772, are precious for the history of Martinism, for it relates the initiation of Saint-Martin (April 17, 1772). We reproduce photographically half of this letter, seeing its importance.

The other half of this letter is in the writing of Saint-Martin, except for the last six lines, and we are now going to analyze it.

The beginning concerns the next departure of the master.

au M. D. L. a. m

G. P. L. Et B. ~n.

Le 17 avril 1772

T P M

Je vous fais part de la nouvelle acquisition
que nous avons faite dans nos C. ⊚ Vertueux
des Gd comp. de ++ ++ &c. après avoir passé
et reconnu nos Emules de fr. Martin et de Serre,
par notre célébration ordinaire et extraordinaire
en conséquence des ordres qui nous ont été donnés
les avons reçus et ordonnés R R ++ en cette
considération incluons sous peine de prévarication
de reconnaître nos fidèles Emules pour tels qu'ils
ont été proclamés dans le ⊚ assurent qu'on
doit être ajouté en tout ce qu'ils professeront
pour ou contre l'avantage de l'ordre et de ses
Emules pour cet effet leur avons délivré quatre
⊚ pour en faire l'usage qu'il convient
selon leurs obligations à quoy ils persistent
En cette considération avons mis nos caractères
ordinaires

Conjoint l'adresse authentique fidèle au P. M. de
fr. Martines D P D L T L C

"I have to inform you of my departure very soon for San Domingo. The reasons that bring me there are to put definitively a solid order into my temporal affairs and to assure a condition for all of my own, in order to then give myself entirely to la Chose for my own satisfaction and that of my emulators. I have in this colony two powerfully rich brothers-in-law, from whom I have good reason to expect considerable relief; they have made me, moreover, in this land, a donation of a great good that I am going to withdraw from the hands of a man who retained it unjustly. I expect that all these affairs will be carried out promptly, and that I will not be a year without seeing France again. I commend myself always to your good prayers, and I ask the eternal that he watches over my days in time immemorial."

We see that these reasons are serious. Thus falls the obscurities which surrounded until the present for the critics this journey of Martinès.

But this whole beginning is in the writing of Saint-Martin; Martinès has taken the pen, without doubt unknown to his secretary, in order to speak again on that famous gown:

Do not draw any grief of your due of the two hundred forty pounds that I owe you for the gown that you were good enough to send to Madame; you will be the first payed upon my return, my letter will serve you as security or guarantee.

Signed: De Pasqually de la Tour.

This signature placed at the bottom of a paper destined to serve as guarantee seems to indicate that it is certainly the legal name of Martinès.

Here the exchanged correspondence is stopped in France, the following letter of October 12, 1773 (that is to say more than a year after the preceding one) is dated from San Domingo and gives us some interesting details on the works of the master during this lapse of time.

"Although some temporal affairs have forced me to stay in the colony, I have never lost sight of la Chose. I have always led the temporal together with the spiritual. By these means I dare to hope that all will go well. The eternal knows my views in the one and the other, he also protects my person by preserving it in perfect health, which will put me in a position to conclude here the affairs of the inheritance that I am claiming in this colony and to return as promptly as possible to France, in order to live in the midst of our spiritual children and to compensate them with interest for lost time."

The master had drawn up, he said, instructions for all the degrees and all the tables.

He then touches on administrative details, speaks on the initiation of the sister of Willermoz, and hopes always for a prompt return to France.

"If it pleases God, I am counting on having ended my temporal affairs in this land towards the end of next year, time when I propose to pass into France, beyond any unforeseen circumstances."

Alas, all these beautiful projects will soon be annihilated!

In ending his letter, the master announces his intention to deposit all his papers into the hands of Master Caignet de Lester, commissioner general of the navy and his cousin.

"The V.P.M. Caignet, who is overwhelmed by the weight of his position, charges me to tell you a thousand things on his part, the ones more beautiful than the others.

"As my intention is to leave in deposit all my originals in his hands for reasons powerful to my knowledge, this is a further reason for you to establish correspondence with him."

"The civil affairs go very slowly here, despite the strength of great protections. Nevertheless, I do not have long to wait for their completion, one way or another."

Willermoz follows the councils of Martinès since we may read at the beginning of this letter the following note:

Received on Saturday, January 29, 1774. - Responded on the 30th. wrote the same day to M. Caignet de Lester.

On April 24, 1774, Martinès addresses from Port-au-Prince a new letter to Willermoz.

First of all, he encourages him on the subject of his experiments; then he touches again on some questions of administrative order and asks him for some information on the subject of an undertaking of the Lodge of France in which the name of W. is found mixed. In short, a purely administrative letter, and with which we will have to occupy ourselves later.

We now come to the last letter of don Martinès, written a month before his death, and dated from Port-au-Prince on August 3, 1774.

This letter begins by the announcement of the sending of the rituals of the Order by the intermediary of the F. Timbale. He then names the V.P.M. Caignet de Lester as Grand M. R.+, charged to receive his spiritual succession in the direction of the Order. Here, then, are some details that interest us more particularly for the moment:

"I am with fever at the moment that I write you this letter of advice, occasioned by two large sores, one in the left arm and the other in the right leg. I am not writing to anyone, being absolutely unable to do so."

DEATH OF THE MASTER

This is the last information given by Martinès concerning his death.

On the back of this letter, we find valuable indications according to the hand of Willermoz.

Dom (with an m) Martinès de Pasqually
from Port-au-Prince on August 3, 1774
Remitted on November 5, 1774 with that of M. Caignet Responded on January 31, 1775

and from another ink,

HE HAS DIED
ON SEPTEMBER 20, 1774
Letters from Dom Martinès
De Pasqually Delatour
Of Bordeaux
Deliveries from 1767 to 1772 and 1774

This information is found confirmed by the precious sheet placed at the front of the correspondence of Martinès and thus worded:

Letters from Dom Martinès de Pasqually
de la Tour of Bordeaux
Delivered from 1767 to 1772 and 1774
HE HAS DIED ON TUESDAY, SEPTEMBER 20, 1774
AT PORT-AU-PRINCE IN AMERICA
He has named the P.M. Caignet de Lester his successor.
He departed from Bordeaux on Nay 5, 1772

∴

Lettres de Dom Martines
de Pasqually Delatour
de Bordeaux Reçues
de 1767, en 1772 & 1774

il est mort le mardi 20 7bre 1774
au Port au Prince en amerique

il a nommé le Sr Caignet
de Lestere son Successeur

il etoit parti de Bordeaux
embarqué le 5 May 1772

Mad. Colas Vve de Pasqually
de Bordeaux du 16 mai 1779

elle nous fait savoir qu'elle va
se remarier avec Mr D'Olabarat
Marie en juillet suivant
Son fils jean anselme né 17 juin 1768
est au college a Lescar pres de Pau.
elle recommande l'abbé fournier

repondu le 12 juin

Finally, we find at the end of the correspondence a letter to madame widow of Martinès that we will know how to better analyze only in reproducing the note from Willermoz, placed at the bottom of this letter.

Madame Colas, widow de Pasqually of Bordeaux on May 14, 1779

She informs us that she is going to get married to M. d'Olabarat; married in the following July.

Her son Jean Anselme born June 17, 1768, is at the college of Lescar near de Pau. She recommends the abbé Fournier.

Responded on June 12.

In truth it must be said that, in her letter Mrs. de Pasqually has given less complete information than W. in his note.

Here, then, is what reaches us in terms of our analysis. We have followed, as best we can, the life of Martinès, from day to day, according to his letters.

CHAPTER II
MAGICAL PRACTICES

DOCTRINE OF MARTINÈS DE PASQUALLY

We have been able to follow the life of Martinès de Pasqually nearly from day to day for seven years. We are now going to occupy ourselves with his doctrine and magical practices, the one being intimately bound to the other.

The documents that we possess are particularly valuable from this point of view, for they allow to completely clarify this side so unknown of the history of Martinism.

We always follow the same plan in our expose, that is to say that we will analyze and cite successively all the letters of Martinès in developing over all the passages which are connected to our study.

Nevertheless, some complementary clarifications are necessary before approaching in detail each of the letters of the master. We are therefore going to summarize in some pages the teachings of the Kabbalah and the esoteric tradition which derives therefrom, concerning the human being and his relationships with the invisible world.

The printed writings and the manuscripts that we possess from the principal disciple of Pasqually: Louis-Claude de Saint Martin, allows us to lay down as a rule the extreme importance of man from the point of view of transcendent knowledge.
Relying on the analogical doctrine of the relationship of the microcosm and macrocosm, Saint-Martin recommends to his disciples "to explain Nature by man, and not man by Nature." This is an application of γνωτι σευτον from Greek philosophy.

But the study of man must not be limited to the physical plane: anatomy and physiology constitute only the study of the *human shell* and would not suffice. The true man is the Spirit-Man and psychology comes closer than any other science to the goals indicated to the disciple by the Martinist masters.

But we must not fall here into a gross error and believe that classical psychology is of great usefulness to a true initiate.

This is at the most a vulgar anatomy of the psychic organs, and the faculties studied by the psychologists are not made into a suitable hierarchy. There exists, moreover, a whole other category of transcendent faculties, vaguely glimpsed under the names of intuition and presentiment, and which require a theoretical and especially *practical* study for which the school cares very little.

Now, in all times there have existed more or less secret fraternities, giving to some men, chosen by progressive initiation, the theory and practice of the transcendent faculties which exist in seed form in the human being. The members of these fraternities: initiates of the great university of Hermes, therapeuts, Essenes, Gnostics, Templars, alchemists, Rose-Croix, etc., etc., preserve always the secret tradition concerning these mysterious faculties of the human being, and were always considered by the true philosophers as men evolved and superior to the others.

But in all times there has also existed a category of men guided by ambition alone, and very little disposed to submit to the trials or to the progressive and demanding examinations, as much of physical courage and mental strength as of intellectual knowledge.

These men, that we find again under different names in every era: vulgar conquerors, persecutors of the Initiates or of the Prophets, Pharisees, ignorant and sectarian bishops of the first Christian centuries, inquisitors and theologians, pseudo-freethinkers, and pseudo-positivists closest to us, always considering the members of the secret fraternities as enemies or madmen, pursuing them by every means: fire, sword, sarcasm.

Well, Martinès de Pasqually belonged to the first category, to the evolved men, to the elect, to those that the authors of the biographical dictionaries call with disdain "*The Illuminati.*"

To illuminate the human being by provoking the human development of the divine faculties dormant within him by matter, such was the aim that Martinès pursued; such was the sole raison d'être of his doctrine which is ever obscure and incomprehensible for the profane, whatever knowledge he may have besides the ordinary philosophy.

What, then, are the consequences of illuminism for the one who confines himself to the practices imposed by the ritual?

What are the means to arrive at this knowledge?

Such are the two questions that we must now resolve.

To the degree that the divine faculties are developed, the mental being is transformed at the expense of the physical appetites. The instinctive satisfactions are reduced to their paltry value, the material motives which move the vulgar men: money, official honors, satisfactions to vanity; all that disappears insensibly, and the point of view under which one considers life changes completely in character. Instead of seeing from low to high, from brutal strength towards the ideal, the initiate or artist (who is an initiate in indistinctive mode) sees from the high to the low, from the Idea, of which he is permeated, towards Matter, which seems imperceptible to him... over there. But if the physical sensation has lost its empire, a wholly special sensibility has been born, with new modes of perception allowing him to acquire new impressions, and to deduce therefrom new certitudes and connections with the invisible world are established, connections always misunderstood by the profane and always incomprehensible to them.

To enter into communication with the invisible, such is the first result obtained by the illuminated.

But this is the great mystery, the secret that must not be delivered as food to the curiosity of the fool; thus, the initiate lets the vulgar masses mock and insult him; to call him in turns charlatan, hallucinating, or even lunatic. He knows what he thinks on the reality of the mysteries, and a disdainful silence is the only countenance that he will oppose to the slanders and insolent scoffing.

The problems which are unsolvable for the philosopher, armed with the great wooden saber of induction, are resolved positively for the illuminated who no longer debate the immortality of the soul since he can disengage at will the divine spark which is within him from the material body that furnishes him the essence for an existence. The reality of the creative forces is no longer a problem for the one who can at will perceive them in action and sometimes participate in their essence. Therefore, the illuminated do not fear death, the majority of the phases of which he has already overcome experientially, any more than the miner fears the corridors of the mine where he descends each day. But this situation of evolved man cannot give the least pride to the one who realizes it, for the evolution of humanity is a collective act, and all the efforts of the one who knows must be devoted to divinizing as much as possible the human phlegm that swarms at his feet. Thus, illuminism implies absolutely the existence of a social collective action, connected with the individual initiatic action.

As to the means to arrive at the development of the transcendent faculties, they are summarized in a triple impetus: alimentary for the physical body; respiratory for the astral body; musical and psychical for the Spirit.[4]

Martinès, an elevated adept of the esoteric tradition, was going to develop all these points in initiating Willermoz progressively; but it is only with a respect mixed with fear that he will speak of this spiritual influence, of this action of the invisible world that the poor disciple of Lyon takes so many years to perceive, of this great mystery always designated under the enigmatic name of "La Chose."

In the first sessions, the new disciples admitted to take part in the works of the master would see "la Chose" accomplishing mysterious actions. They would leave from there enthusiastic and terrified, like Saint-Martin, or drunk with pride and ambition like the disciples of Paris. Some apparitions were produced, some strange beings, of an essence different from terrestrial human nature, took turns speaking and uttered profound teachings, and each disciple is called to reproduce alone and by himself the same phenomena.

The experiments begin; but they want to go too quickly, they want to avoid the fatiguing training, and all fail. Then they accuse the master, they lay the blame on Martinès for their failure and dissatisfaction, and Martinès responds very sincerely: "But, my beloved Master, if it was me who directed the invisible world, my greatest ambition would have been to satisfy you. But what can I tell you? 'La Chose' requires sure and very serious proofs of a limitless devotion. On the day that you will be worthy, the phenomena will come."

This is indeed what is produced, and we must praise without reserve the obstinacy of Willermoz who put more than ten years into obtaining convincing facts, whereas at the end of two or three years of study, the majority of the other disciples were satisfied.

The practices taught by Martinès derive uniquely from ceremonial magic, as we will see later. Let us point out, however, the considerable importance attributed by the master to the "Luminaries," the candles arranged in the circle. This is indeed a very original characteristic of the Martinist tradition.

The preceding notions were, in our opinion, indispensable for understanding the extracts that are going to follow. We will add, at the occasion, all the complementary developments that seem necessary to us.

Initiation of Willermoz

The initiation practice of Willermoz begins on August 13, 1768, by a letter of four pages in-8vo, from which we separate the following passage, having reference to the alimentary regimen and to the first astrological concepts.

DIET - ASTROLOGICAL CORRESPONDENCES – PRAYERS

August 13, 1768.

"As regards what you must do and the life that you must keep for your spiritual and temporal functions; for the temporal, I would tell you nothing other than the prohibition that I gave you on temporal aliments, which is that you will no longer eat during your life the blood of any species of animals, nor will you eat domestic pigeon, nor will you eat any species of kidneys, nor the fat from any kind of animals.

"You will carefully fast for the time that you will be ordered at each equinox; you will begin your fast the day before you want to work your quarter circle; you cannot, nor should you, work in your capacity of apprentice R.+ except three days following the beginning of the equinoxes. You will follow the moon of March and that of September, and not the days that they have fixed to be the equinox, not using the ordinary days nor the month which fixes them, but rather the lunar star; for this you will observe the moon of March and that of September. You will never forget your daily office of the Holy Spirit. If you wish to follow it later with the operation of the apostles, neither will you forget to say the Miserere mei at the center of your chamber, in the evening before you go to sleep, facing towards the angle which faces the rising sun; then you will say the De Profundis, kneeling on both knees and face prostrated to the ground. The Miserere mei is said standing on your feet. If you have other daily prayers to make according to your custom, you may make them, but those that I order you are indispensible, just as the regimen of life."

As we can see, these are Catholic prayers that Martinès employs in his operations.

We note, moreover, that as a true magician, the master attaches a very great importance to the astronomical and astrological data. It is only at the time of the equinoxes that the first operations take place, and again it is quite necessary to observe the situation of the moon, as shows the letter of September 2, 1768, giving some complementary information.

ASTROLOGICAL DATA – PRAYERS

"September 2, 1768.

"It is the moon of September which guides us; we have then its first quarter until full to work, that is to say by beginning four or five days before its fullness.

"As to the keeping of your spiritual obligations, you will personally say the Office of the Holy Spirit, the *Miserere mei*, and the *De Profundis* once per week which is on Thursday at the sign and day of Jupiter, just as David used for his reconciliation that I will instruct you on later. Then you will know the value and the strength of this prayer. You say the Office of the Holy Spirit in one hour of the day; I will not limit you at all; but for the *Miserere mei* and the *De Profundis*, you say them in the evening before going to sleep, the De Profundis with face against the ground, the Miserere standing facing towards the orient.

"You will be entirely informed on all the points that you ask of me concerning our work and yours, eight days, or five days in advance in order to put yourselves in order. The manner to place the candles will likewise be sent. You will purchase a little ritual in order to have the prayers of the benedictions and exorcisms that I will indicate to you when I write to these ends."

ON THE MAGICAL CIRCLE

After these fundamental ideas we approach the practice of the magical circle that we are going to see developed later on. Some clarifications are indispensible in order to dispel as much as possible the obscurity inherent in such questions.

In every experiment of ceremonial magic, the operator isolates himself from the exterior milieu by means of a circle traced upon the ground and containing some mystical names which, according to tradition, have a great influence over the invisible world.

Generally, one makes three concentric circles at the center of which one draws a cross whose branches reach the largest circle, which divides each of the three circles into four segments, each at one of the cardinal points. In each of these segments one draws the mystical names corresponding analogically to the powers of each of the cardinal points.[5]

Martinès has modified this ritual very slightly in order to constitute each of these degrees.

After having inspected the different passages of his letters, and in absence of any explicative drawing, we think that the ritual of the master was as follows.

Instead of tracing a complete circle, the Apprentice traced only the segment or *quarter circle* corresponding to the Orient.

This segment was traced in the EAST corner of the chamber of operation. It was delimited by half of the vertical branch and half of the horizontal branch of the great central cross.

Beyond this quarter circle (*containing* perhaps itself another small circle) one traced at the West corner of the chamber of operation a circle called by Martinès the *circle of retreat.* A small circle could also, but optionally, be contained in a quarter of the great circle.

In short, a quarter circle in the East, a circle in the West, separated from one another by a space of two feet, such seems to me to be the ritual of the first personal operations.

In case of error on my part, the reader may correct it by meditating on the following letters:

THE EQUINOXES

"Letter of September 11, 1768.

"I write you for the first and last time on our mysterious equinoxal year which is comprised from one equinox to the other, to notify you to be at your East angle of observation on the 27, 28, and 29 of the present month of September in order to receive there your sympathetic ordination of virtue and power relative to your worthiness and quality of R.+."

THE CIRCLE OF RETREAT AND THE QUARTER CIRCLE

You are notified in the name of the Eternal to find yourself prostrated in the circle which is in the West where the word IAB is written, precisely at midnight from the 27th to the 28th. Make sure that you will make this prostration only after having traced entirely all the attributes which are in your quarter circle, beginning with the figure and finishing with all that is generally dependent on it, such as you have been given at Paris. You will place three candles at the angle of your quarter circle; one inside the circle which is in your quarter circle on the bar written RAP; you put likewise two candles at each extremity of your quarter circle and one at the center of the quarter in the middle of the second line which divides the names; and the hieroglyphs which are written there within; this sole light is the symbol of my sympathetic presence at your operations. The circle where you must make your prostration will be at two feet of distance from the west angle which faces the East angle where your quarter circle will be traced. After this preparation is done you will make your prostration and dress.

ATTIRE

You will be attired above with a short jacket, breeches, and black stockings, divested of any metal; not even a pin upon you; you will not even have your shoes on your feet during your prostration; but you will wear them slipshod during your invocations since it is necessary for you to be fixed; if it were possible to be more perfectly in order, you will have made for yourself shoes and hat with a sole of cork in order to have nothing in the place or upon you unclean or impure, here is why they call Pope's slippers; you must understand me. Then you will have over your first attire a long white robe, around which it will have a large border the color of fire about a foot wide, and around the sleeves which are made in the fashion of an alb; there will likewise be a border the color of fire about a half-foot; there will likewise be around the collar of said robe, a lining of the same color, outside of the said collar about five fingers across; you will have further upon you all the colors of the Order, namely, the celestial blue cord in-saltire at the neck without any attribute; then the black cord passed from right to left, then the red sash from right to left around as a belt, below the abdomen; then you pass the aqua-green sash from left to right over the chest. The placement of these sashes upon your body makes allusion to the material, animal, and spiritual separations.

THE PROSTRATIONS

Being thus vested, you will withdraw the light that is lit in your circle of prostration; you will place it on your right, outside of said circle; then you prostrate yourself inside, completely stretched out chest to ground, and you will rest your forehead upon your two closed fists. This prostration will last without complaint six minutes taken from the time of your ordination of virtue. Then you will raise yourself upright, and you will go light all the candles which were in your circle of prostration without doubt that it will be by the new fire, and when all is lit you will go to make your prostrations in your quarter circle by arranging the two candles which are there inside the two extremities of the quarter circle; and when you will pronounce some of the names which are traced, you will ask God by virtue of the power that he has given to his servants such and such while naming the names written in the angle+ the grace that you ask of him from a sincere heart, truly contrite and submissive, and that in order to assure you his mercy, he will have repeated for you the hieroglyph or some of the hieroglyphs that you will have traced before you, with the white chalk in the middle of the chamber between your quarter circle and your circle of retreat which is in the west where you will always be placed when you wish to work in the future until the time that I will change the work for you which will be more advantageous and more lucrative for you, perhaps, than that of an Apprentice. After your two prostrations you will raise the words from the two circles, just as those which are around the quarter circle, the knees straight and the two hands squared, flat on the ground, you will say while raising three words: in quali que die N..., N..., N... invocavero te velociter exaudi me. After you will have done all these things, you will take your perfumes that you put in a little earthenware dish in which there will be the coal lit with the new fire and you will go to perfume your quarter circle in the east and your circle of retreat which is in the west.

ON THE PERFUMES

Equal parts of:
Saffron.
Male incense.
Flowers of sulphur.
Black and white poppy seeds.
Cloves.
Canella in rods.

Gum mastic in teardrop form.
Sandarac.
Nutmeg.
Mushroom spores.

Mix it all together and then throw a good pinch of it unto the aforesaid dish; then pass it in the form of a circle around the quarter circle; then put again three good pinches of said perfume into said dish where is the new fire and cense four times the west angle. After performing this ceremony, you will make the invocations that I will send to you by the first post, having absolutely no time to transcribe them for you...being pressed to have done some repairs that the last storm has done to my father-in-law's home.

You will observe for the three days of the operation to say in the morning your Office of the Holy Spirit, in the evening, in the chamber where you will work, the Seven Psalms and the Litany of the Saints. You will enter into your laboratory two hours before the hour of midnight, in order to be able to retrace everything anew.

DURATION OF THE OPERATION

The first days of your operation you will not come out of your circle of retreat until one-thirty, nearly two hours after midnight; you will observe to dine on this day at precisely noon and to finish eating at one o'clock sharp. You will not partake of any more food until you have finished your operation. You will be able to drink some water if your have need; but absolutely no coffee or liquor. This is an apt summary of what you must do.

ON THE CANDLES - ON THE OPENING OF THE CIRCLES

Letter of October 2, 1768.

"I have sent you a small triangular talisman which you will return from one point to the other during your work of three days. - As to the situation of your apartment, it is better that you support yourself in the west in order to place your quarter circle, to the north in the future.

"The candles of representation are placed between the circumference of the quarter circle.

"The candle that is to remain alone lit is that which is at the center of your quarter circle that you transport to your angle of retreat or circle of correspondence; as to the other candles, you have them very well placed.

"It is common and even ordained and prescribed by oath that each chief principal sovereign of the circles of divine spiritual operation will hold its circles open by quarter, by half, and the whole year open in order to be in a position to not be at all surprised and fall into deficiency, whether for its particular usefulness, for the Order, for the particular and general instructions, for some sicknesses, and for the propagation of the order and the preservation of its faithful members."

FOLLOWING THE INITIATION (1770)

Here is the ritual of the first operations.

It is necessary to report to us in two years time (February 1770) in order to recover the continuation of practical teachings with some new modifications concerning a more elevated initiatic degree.

There is no longer here a circle of retreat at the west, but a great circle at the center of the chamber and the usual quarter circle in the east.

Here are two very important letters on this subject. One finds among other information the character of the apparitions.

ON THE CIRCLES

"Letter of February 16, 1770.

"You will make a circle with the white chalk in the middle of your chamber, you will also trace your C.O.C. towards the east angle, which will be usual. This done, you will prostrate yourself entire face in the circle that you will have made at the center of your chamber, the aforesaid circle will be about six feet in diameter, the top of your head being while prostrating facing the East angle where will be marked the quarter circle; you will prostrate yourself on the 22nd of next month, day of the Equinox, in order to receive your ordination at precisely ten o'clock at night; and you will remain prostrated for nearly half an hour face down. And I myself will be in my angle at precisely nine o'clock at night in order to work for myself and for you. I will remain in this position until one hour after midnight. When you will have remained the hour indicated in your prostration, you will go extinguish your ordinary lights which are in your quarter circle, you will erase all that you will have traced, and you will withdraw unto yourself.

"On the 25th of said month of next March, you will retrace exactly the same things that you will have done for your ordination, that is to say circle of C.O.C. You will have already made your tracing at eleven o'clock at night precisely; all being ready, you will begin by the last invocations that I have sent you. After you will follow your ordinary work; first you will observe to not place any candle at the center of your circle, which will be drawn in the middle of your chamber; you will trace there the letter that I mark for you in my letter; the said word will be between your legs during the whole time of your work. You will work during your three days the last package that I have sent you, although this work is only for Wednesday and Saturday; the circumstance where you are forces me to have you fall back upon this work during the three days of your operation; no matter the days. To the great ills, great remedies.

"The last work that I have sent you, you will use it after this last operation, all the days that are properly indicated to you by said package; you can do it every week, every month, or two or three times per year, conforming to your will when you will feel rather disposed to doing the work.

"For the future you will not draw any tracing, nor circle, nor any other thing, since this operation may be done in all places without any other form of process."

ON THE VISIONS

The visions are white, blue, clear light red; finally, they are mixed or all white, flame color from white candle, you will see some sparks, you will feel gooseflesh all over your body, all this announces the beginning of the traction that la Chose makes with the one who works. Try, V.B.Mtr., to procure for yourself some of these things, seeing as simple emulators that I have under the ordination of Grand Architect see it night and day, without light nor candle nor any other fire; this does not surprise me at all of them because they are entirely given to la Chose and well ordered; in this they have passed to you their certificates of vision made and signed by their own hand so that you will be convinced of their success in the Order; you will make sure to have them passed to the P. Master substitute so that he sees clearly the success of these Rble. Mtres.; they are the first four: the brother d'Hauterive, the old gentleman captain du Roy, another is the brother Defore the second captain of the artillery, and the other the brother Defournier, old townsman living on his income at Bordeaux, nephew of the grand prior of the Augustines of Paris. If the brother Baron de Calvimon was here, he would likewise have given his certificate, but he will give it to me upon his return from his lands. If others were necessary there would be those of the Venerable brothers *Cabory*, *Schild*, *Marcadi*; these last are in the same case as the first. Here, P. Mtr., are some rather instructed and enlightened persons who would not wish to deceive la Chose, nor to deceive men of good faith by illusions, nor to be deceived themselves.

In the name of the Great Architect of the Universe

Joy, peace, and Blessings be on who hears me,

From the Grand Orient of orients. Bordeaux, L.M.

333-357-579-2448, 5729, of the w. 45 of Christ E.V. 1770 of the second and last quarter of the second moon, this March 13.

"V.R.M.

"I am responding to all your questions: 1st, the placement of the candles are perfectly well placed by the number of ten, and by the number of eight, - you may follow exactly the illumination that you mark for me in your quarter circle, and you will not change anything to this illumination. The candle placed at the West outside of the quarter circle ought to be withdrawn and even a little obscured, in order to allow freedom to the things that must appear free of all elementary light, since the things bear their light with them, - whether white, red, or otherwise, according to what I have marked for you by my last letters.

"The illumination of the East must be well-lighted when you perform the contemplations and let there be absolutely only the sole aforesaid light in the West. You will see to extinguish your lights beginning with those that are at the base of the quarter circle, beginning with the two which are towards the South, marked by the letters MR, after having erased the word. Then you are going to extinguish those which are towards the North, marked by the letters WG. From there you are going to extinguish the two candles which are in the interior of the two rays which are at the top of the angle projecting towards the East, always beginning by pronouncing the word which is inscribed, erase it with your hand, and extinguish the candle. One always begins in the south to extinguish, that is to say by the letters OZ, then you are going to extinguish in the same manner the one which is at the other extremity marked by the letters IA. Then you are going to extinguish in the same custom that which is entirely in the East angle just as you will have done for the others. This done, you will come to place yourself in the great circle, which is in the middle of your quarter circle, where is marked the letters RAP, you will raise all the words which are traced around said circle, beginning by raising the one which gives to the West at the letters IA. Then you are going to raise the one that goes to the South and from there the one which is in the North, and then the one which is to the East; these four raised words which signify to you the four celestial regions and those who direct them spiritually. This done, you will take in hand the candle which is at the Center of the aforesaid circle for your Invocations and place the word to mark by the letters RAP between your legs, and then you will make all your invocations whatsoever. This done, you will erase the word RAP, extinguish the candle, and come to place yourself in the circle of retreat, standing upright, having your face turned toward the East in order to make your observation, and you will have between your legs, the word marked by the letters IAB. You will observe that the candle which is placed in the circle of retreat is the one that you are to hide: the time having come for you to withdraw, you will replace the candle that you had withdrawn to its same circle as it was before; you will raise the words which are around said circle, as well as the one of the Center, by the same manners and ceremonies that you have done with those which are around the great circle which is at the center of your quarter circle. The candle which represents me will be extinguished after the invocations made, while saying: 'Blessed be the one who assists me and who hears me, *O Bagniakim*, Amen.' One will see to raise any words whatsoever while kneeling on the right knee, the left knee raised; one will then see to lighting a candle by the one that burns in the circle of retreat, before it is extinguished, in order to have some light in order to do what one will judge suitable, - this last light, placed in the circle of retreat, being the one which is to serve for the observation of the passes, and having consecrated there a word, it must be extinguished like the others, in order to perform the dismissal of the Spirit which is attached to it. The stars which are high upon the wall of the East and the West should not be put in a circle, they must be traced quite simply with the letters which surround them. As regards the circle which must serve you for the ordination, it will be placed between the circle of retreat and the two rays of your quarter circle; you will observe for this day to move back your circle of retreat and to narrow your quarter circle in order to place there the circle of five feet eight inches in diameter, your height not being six feet. It is of the greatest necessity that your body be exactly enclosed within a circle, this is why they put six feet rather than below for the ordinations.

"You will find marked in your same page the place set where you must place the circle of ordination.

"When you will have lit all the candles of your work, you will recite your seven Psalms of David, then you will perfume your circle of retreat three times; from there you are going to cense the two small circles which are at the bottom of the quarter circle marked by the letters MR by three censings at each; you will do as much at the two others which are at the base of said quarter circle to the North, marked by the letters WG. Then you are going to cense the circle which is at the center of the quarter circle marked by the letters RAP three times like with the others; then you are going to make the same censings at the two small circles above the aforesaid angle, beginning with the one that is marked by the letter Z; then at the one that is marked by the letters IA, three times like all the others, then you will give four censings at the small circle which is positively in the aforesaid angle of said quarter circle marked by the letter IW: which will make in all twenty-eight censings which will produce the mysterious number ten. The circle of prostration and the letters of the word that you must use for your ordination is marked at the base of your quarter circle just as you will see and such as you will execute.

"I am informing you that I am going to work for the general re-establishment of the health of my wife, having already worked at it for more than twelve days, having obtained only a very weak glimmer of her healing. I recommend her to your work in order to obtain all together from the Eternal her perfect reestablishment; her illness being most curious and without fever. As regards the certificates that I have sent you, there is not any suspicion of illusion, directly or indirectly, nor variation, nor change of time of day, nor of season which may persuade and convince the aforesaid subjects to allow themselves to be amazed by illusory things nor by sophistical words; they bear some facts which will appear to you even more amazing than the journals since I have made use of their same journals which have been very successful for me in research that I have made and that I have interpreted very well on events present and future, which have performed for me very perfectly with success by the grace of the Great A. of the U. You will begin your prostrations before perfuming; the first is made in the circle of retreat, the second at the letters MR, the third at the letters WG, the fourth at the letters RAP, the fifth at the letter z, the sixth at the letters IA and the seventh at the letters IW. After the prostrations you will perfume as I have told you. This is all that I may say to you R.M. concerning what you ask me, having very little time to give myself for your instruction. Keep yourself ready for the 22nd of the present month, 25, 26, 27th also of the present month. What is done at the South is very good. You will begin by Ex[orcism] an Exc[onjurati]on towards Monday which will be made immediately after, before the invocation where the order will be followed where will be placed the aforesaid Exc[onjurati]on in the invocations. You told me that you had to return to Paris, around the month of next April, when the president M. de Grainville must likewise return in order to make definitive arrangements for the general good of the Order; this is what I ardently desire. And may the Eternal bless your undertaking in everything for this subject. I will contribute no less by my next working so that he deigns to favor you as much spiritually as temporally and keep you for a time immemorial in his retinue. Amen+++.

"D.M. De Pasqualis
G.S."

I have sent off your letter for the P.M. Grainville, the name of the M. Conf. is called M. de Grivau, captain of infantry.

Dom Martinez at Bordeaux
on March 13, 1770.
Explanation given of the 1/4 Circle
For the 22-25, 26, 27 of March.
In sending me my drawing.

There are thus some very curious details on this Martinist ritual which we know until the present so poorly in the profane world.

Willermoz never obtains any interesting practical results. It is not the same for the master, who on April 7, 1770, gives the following details on an operation that he had made to heal his wife.

HEALING OF THE WIFE OF MARTINÈS BY A MAGICAL OPERATION

"August 7, 1770.

"I will grant you then, P.M., part of the grace that I have obtained from God, by the strength of my works and the legitimate sincere prayers of my disciples and emulators in the Order. I have not delayed long at all to feel the efficacious effects of the grace that the Eternal has been willing to grant me in favor of re-establishing the health of my wife that death surrounded by its most pale colors while surrounding the corporeal form of my wife with the most fearful ailments which are susceptible to reducing the individual of the human nature to its reintegration by force, against the prescriptions of the duration of its course.

"I am going to make to you a sincere confession of the different ailments which overwhelm my wife. You will tremble at hearing them pronounced. 1st, the dissolution of the blood. 2nd, loss of blood for 54 days. 3rd, obstruction of the uterus. 4th, a loosening of all the intestinal parts. 5th, a nephritic colic, a swelling of the glands which are at the right side of the groin. And at last definitively a painful rheumatic sciatica. Consultations made with all the celebrated physicians and surgeons of our town, done in the presence of the whole family, of my wife, and in the presence of 7 or 8 of my emulators, who despite all their prescriptions condemned my wife to certain death, which grieved her whole family. After having received this cruel sentence, I gave a report of the different ailments that overcame my wife, which surprised them a little, and they responded to me that they abandoned her to my experience, they having never seen this. The sick never having had any fever, this had greatly disoriented them, and I charge myself with the help of God to see to the entire recovery of my patient. The said doctors ordered my wife to submit to my prescriptions, though they do not believe that I will bring her through this affair.

"Briefly on the 3rd day of my work, I saw the sign of her healing in which I perceived truly what danger she was in just as the faculty had condemned her. An efficacious proof of the grace that I have received was that on the fourth day of my work, I lifted my wife and jostled her a little which made an abscess burst that she had in her lower abdomen, which rendered a quantity of frightful matter; this abscess today is still in suppuration by the ways of ordinary nature; this suppuration is made today as a white loss.

"This prompt healing made quite a din in our town and in our province."

Following this communication, Martinès gives again to his disciples the following practical counsels and announces new magical works.

LA CHOSE

"January 20, 1770.

"I think that you ought not doubt anything that I advance to you, on the contrary, I exhort you to follow my advice and allow yourself to be led by the one who is truly attached to you, just as you must judge it by the things included that I send you in order to prepare you for la Chose which you desire to know. The grace that I ask of you is not to speak to a living soul concerning what I have not yet had passed to anyone, not even to any of my R.+, knowing it is not yet their time to be able to withdraw themselves a little from the greater world in order to be able to give themselves entirely to la Chose. Truly, if la Chose was not such as I assure, and had it not manifested as it has done, whether before me or before so many persons who have wished to know it, I would have abandoned it myself; but I would have removed therefrom in conscience all those who would have wished to approach it in good faith."

LA CHOSE

"April 7, 1770.

"As regards the success that you have not yet received from la Chose, this must not alarm you. La Chose is difficult for those who desire it too ardently before their time. Be steadfast, you will be rewarded while you think the least on it.

"I do not hide at all, powerful M., that it is necessary for a true R.+ to be removed from all impure matter, and especially that of fornication which brings dissention to the soul.

I recommend to you to follow exactly what the G.M. de Grainville will tell you concerning the Order; I will order him to have you work in the four circles with the four circles of correspondence. You will do the invocations yourself or with him, it is all the same."

ON THE INVOCATION

"When the convalescence of my wife will allow me, I am going to work on the different invocations that are necessary for the 7 operating days of the week, each bearing on the good geniuses of the planets and their major chief ruling over them. I have begun this work; it is very satisfying and curious. I have left the interests of the Order in the hands of the P.M. de Grainville. After this working I will make the invocations for all the operations of each month, of each equinox with the exception of the two solstices."

The following year (1771) at the approach of the equinoxes, the loyal disciple of Lyon asks again about some new technical information that Martinès sent him. Saint-Martin is then the master's secretary; for the letter is in the writing of the future initiate, and the orthography is perfect.

ASTRAL INFLUENCES - THE MOON

"November 16, 1771.

"It will be quite possible for you, Beloved Master, to set for me a month in advance, according to your desires, the time when you will be able to work in your equinoxes; I am likewise leaving you the choice of the three consecutive days which will be most convenient for you within a period of eight days, that I will have presented you; thus the difficulty will never come from my side; but I cannot respond to you that it is the same as yours. As I am only leading you by the laws of Nature, I am obliged to govern myself on the lunar course for my work here below because it is the star which principally directs the inferior part, and I have not yet made any calculation in order to know at what time will fall the moon of next march. When I will have assured myself, I will take great care to inform you thereof, but I repeat to you, it may very well be that its time does not agree with your own. I know that it will be difficult for you to occupy yourself with spiritual work from March 20 until April 5. You will be free before the term; inform me if you also know it after, because it may be that the equinoxal moon goes up into the month of April."

THE WORK OF THE THREE DAYS

"Let us suppose the article of time arranged and let us speak on the kind of work that you will have to do. I believe to have informed you to not think at all yet on the one that M. de Grainville has given you, and to preserve it for a time when you will have made more progress. My intention has been and is that you limit yourself to the work of three days that I have sent back to you from here, all translated from the Latin into French. You will join to this the invocation of the G.A. that you have, by following exactly the instruction that I have already sent you on this subject. The grand invocation of midnight does not belong to this last work; thus, this object is not pressing. As to the particular invitations and convocations, I believe to have already transmitted to you something that is connected to it, and the matter will be easy to fulfill, especially as the operant may put there his own, provided that it tends always to the good."

The operation was, alas, no more successful than the others for Willermoz, and the following year the failure occurred again.

Nevertheless, the master gives great hope in one of his last letters written at Port-au-Prince on May 9, 1772:

HOPE FOR AN IMMINENT SUCCESS

"May 9, 1772.

"I share greatly in the mortification to have had so little success; I have foreseen by my working that if you have had in your own any satisfaction that it was not considerable; but I nevertheless recognize something that is here:

"I cannot even doubt that this has passed in all or in part with you, though you have seen nothing. If you had been able to fix there the least characteristic, or only perceive it in the suddenness of the pass, it would have been for you a great guide which would serve you to discover the rest, for it will never be but by yourself and by your own intelligence that you will succeed in instructing and forming yourself, either in the work or in the interpretation. It is nevertheless not necessary to alarm yourself by what is so rigorous and so unmanageable for you; this ought, on the contrary, to redouble your courage and your confidence in the certitude that your time and your success cannot fail to arrive if you will it, for in the end, man is their master."

This letter gives us a very important detail, namely that the practice includes two parts;

1. *The working* or magical operation destined to bring forth visions.
2. *The interpretation* of these visions, the key of the symbols employed by the invisible world to communicate with the initiate.

Before passing, then, to the exposition of the doctrine of Martinès, let us stop yet for a few moments on these practices.

First of all, a question that is posed by the continual successive failures of Willermoz is that of knowing whether the "visions" exist and if Martinès has given proofs before other disciples than the merchant of Lyon?

On this point the critic seems to have clarified the question very well. Mr. Franck, in his remarkable book on Martinism, invokes indeed two witnesses, that of Saint-Martin and that of the abbé Fournier; here are the two passages concerning this question.

"I will not hide from you at all that in the school I have passed through, more than twenty-five years ago, the *communications* of every kind were numerous and frequent, that I have had my share thereof like all the others, and that, in this share, all the indicative signs of the Repairer were included."

(*Saint-Martin, cit. by Franck*, p. 17.)

The abbé Fournier informs us, on the faith of his own experience, that Martinès had the gift to *confirm* (this is a stock word in the school) to confirm his teachings by the lights from on high, by exterior visions, at first vague and rapid as lightning, then more and more distinct and prolonged.

(Franck, p. 18.)

But another extract from the letters of Saint-Martin, cited by Franck, gives us again new and curious details on this subject:

ON THE POWERS

"If the enumeration of the powers and the necessity of these classes is a new domain for you, the friend B (Boehme) will procure for you great relief on these subjects. The school through which I passed has given us also in this genre a good nomenclature. There are extracts thereof in my works, and I am content to summarize here my ideas on these two nomenclatures. That of B. is more substantial than ours; ours is more brilliant and more detailed, but I do not believe it as profitable, especially as the language of the land is not, so to speak, necessary to conquer it, and that it ought not be the object of warriors to speak languages but rather to subdue the rebellious nations. Finally, that of B. is more divine, ours is more spiritual; that of B. may do all for us if we know how to identify ourselves with it, ours demands a practical and decisive operation which renders the fruits thereof more uncertain and perhaps less durable, that is to say that ours is turned towards the operations in which our master was strong, whereas that of B. is entirely turned towards plenitude of the divine action that ought to hold in us the place of the other."

(*St. Martin, unpublished correspondence cited by Franck*, p. 24.)

It will suffice finally to report on the "certificates" given by Martinès to Willermoz in his correspondence in order to be certain that many of the disciples obtained some very important practical results.

But the archives that we possess permit us to give to the question posed to us a rather unexpected response. Willermoz succeeds in his goals and obtains phenomena of the highest importance, which reach their apogee in 1785, that is to say *thirteen years* after the death of his initiator Martinès de Pasqually.

We may follow in the correspondence from Willermoz and from Saint-Martin (1771 to 1790) the appearance and the progress of these practical results which incite Saint-Martin to come several times to Lyon, and we possess moreover a part of the papers as well as the catalog of teachings given by the apparition that W. designates under the name of "*the Unknown Agent charged with the work of initiation*."

We see what constancy was necessary for Willermoz to obtain serious results, and one remains astonished at the obstinacy displayed on this occasion by the one who, more than any other, may be called "the man of desire."

We have now ended the exposition of the "ritual" employed by the Martinists.

The readers who are current on the theory and practice of magic will understand the strictly traditional character of this ritual.

The addition of the "luminaries" is, however, characteristic of Martinism. The profanes will see here only charlatanism, hallucination, and madness. This matters little, however, to the truth of these facts which will only be well known in fifty years; until then the profanes have the right to profane the mysteries, and disdainful silence ought to be the sole response of the initiates.

But we learn here these burning subjects and approach now the study of the doctrine proper of the founder of Martinism.

THE DOCTRINE

Of the three successive principles studied by esotericism: God, Man, and the Universe, it is upon man that Martinès principally bears his attention.

We have, moreover, already insisted upon this subject at the start of this chapter.

But of all the ideas concerning man and his evolution, nothing interests Martinès more than that of the fall and rehabilitation, which he calls reintegration. Mr. Franck even gives in his work some pages of a treatise dedicated by the master to this question.

1. The fall has been universal for all the material beings, and the reintegration will be too.
2. Man is the divine agent of this reintegration.
3. "The perverse being" himself will be reintegrated through love.

Such are the three fundamentals of the doctrine of Martinès on this point.

"According to the doctrine of Martinès Pasqualis, man is not the only being who bears within him the traces and who suffers the consequences of a first error; all the beings are fallen like him; those who populate the heavens or who surround the throne of eternity, as those who are exiled upon this earth. All feel with sorrow the evil that keeps them far from their divine source, and impatiently await the day of their reintegration." (*Franck*, p. 13&14.)

"Martinès Pasqualis had the active key of all that our beloved Boehme sets forth in his theories; but he did not believe us to be in a state to bear these high virtues. He therefore had some points that our friend Boehme had not known or had not wished to show, such as the redemption of the perverse being with which the *first man* would have been charged to labor."

(*Saint-Martin, cited by Franck*, p. 15.)

We find here the so admirable theory developed later by Fabre d'Olivet. (*La langue hébraique restituée, Cain.*)

The state of the Savior, of Christ, is a state accessible to every human soul acting in absolute concert with the providential principles.

Now, here is what the abbé Fournier assures us to have learned from the mouth of Pasqually:

"Each of us, in walking in his tracks, may be elevated to the degree attained by Jesus Christ. It is for having done the will of God that Jesus Christ, clothed in human nature, has become the Son of God himself. In imitating his example or in conforming our will to the divine will, we will enter like him into the eternal Union of God. We will empty ourselves of the spirit of Satan in order to permeate ourselves with the divine spirit; we will become one as God is one, and we will be consumed in the eternal unity of God the Father, of God the Son, and of God the Holy Spirit, and consequently consumed in the enjoyment of the eternal and divine delights."

(*Franck*, p. 14.)

It is by the enlightened resignation to the "evils that destiny brings along with it" that man attains to this evolution, powerfully aided by the magical operations which permit the objective assistance of a guide come from the invisible world.

Such is, summarized in so many lines, the doctrine set forth in detail by Martinès in the following extracts from his letters, and that Ad. Franck has determined very well.

"We now possess, in its most essential elements, the doctrine of Martinès Pasquallis. It is comprised of two very distinct parts: the one inner, speculative, spiritual, to which are attached ancient traditions, if it was not entirely within the traditions themselves; the other exterior, practical, up to a certain point material or at least symbolic, which depended, as Saint-Martin informs us, completely on a system of the hierarchy of virtues and powers, or the degrees of the spiritual world interposed between God and man."[6]

We are now going to cite the principal passages connected to the doctrine in the letters of Martinès.

On September 19, 1767, with respect to his illness, Martinès made the following reflection:

FEEBLENESS AND GREATNESS OF MAN

We are all men, and in this quality, none of us are righteous before Him (God); we recall that he has not put us upon this surface for him, but rather for ourselves. It remains with us to be with him, as it is in our power to remain with ourselves alone.

God has punished me by striking me in this way; but his just chastisement ought to reassure the same man on his doubts. He was never similar to the beast in that the beast remains unpunished, and man is punished by the eternal when he falls, and the punishment that man receives, the moment that he has sinned, assures him of the goodness of that perfect being; not wishing to lose him entirely, he afflicts him and makes him see by that, that he has not at all removed from him his mercy and his grace.

Man is ambitious, curious, and insatiable. His imagination takes the place of his thought, his weakness and his disgust destroys in an instant the action of his projects, which renders him disquieted, wicked, and evil against those who have wished to raise him up; admitting no other success than by the one who directs them in his operations, placing an incomparable confidence in him, taking him even for a god in their request, and even ignoring that this is only a man like them. As for me, I am man and I do not believe to have within me more than another man. I have always said that every man had before him all the suitable materials to do all that I have been able to do, in my small part. Man has only to will, he will have power and ability.

PRACTICE - STATE AND REINTEGRATION OF MAN

"April 13, 1768.

Do not be impatient, wait for your time, these kinds of things are not at the sole disposition of man; but rather at that of the M.H. and A.-P. Eternal. It would be to speak to you rashly and impertinently, if I told you that these things are in my sole power. I am only a weak instrument of which God is willing, unworthy though I may be, to make use of me, in order to recall men, my equals, to their first state of Mason which means spiritually man or soul, in order to make them see truly that they are actually Man-God, being created in the image and in the resemblance of that All-Powerful Being.

AIM OF THE ORDER - MAN OF DESIRE

In regard to what you told me, that you wish to be absolutely convinced truly of the aim of the Order, it depends on you yourself; do your best, God and the one who is charged with your conduct in this subject will meet you half-way. The Order contains a true science; it is founded upon the pure and simple truth; it is impossible for sophistry to reign there and for charlatanism to preside there; on the contrary, the false has only a time, it flees, and the truth remains. In order to be able to convince you of this truth, it would be necessary for you to follow me for a very long time, closer than you have done, and by these means all your doubts would be dissipated.

You possess upon yourself all the emblems of this pure truth. Only observe the five unequal digits that you have on your hands and feet, seek a little to divine these different emblems. I swear to you that you will no longer have any great thing to ask of me in order to be sure that the Order contains for the minor of this lower world things most necessary and essential for his advantage. Thus, the order seeks the *man of desire*, and when he lets himself be led, he is content.

THE "PREDECESSORS"

Here, V.P.M., is all that I am able to respond on all the questions that you posed to me in your letter. I am responding without concealment and without flattery.

I have never sought to lead anyone into error, nor to deceive the persons who have come to my good faith in order to partake in some of the knowledge that my predecessors[7] have transmitted to me. I will prove always before God and contrary men, and even for those who are my most cruel enemies.

(Here is the key to the problem of the "five unequal digits" given by Martinès to his disciples.)

THE HUMAN HAND

"May 5, 1769.

Through the power of commandment, man was still able to bind them (the evil demons) in privation, in refusing them all communication with him, which is represented to us by the unequalness of the five digits of the hand, of which the middle finger represents the soul, the thumb the good spirit, the index the good intellect; the other two fingers represent likewise the demoniacal spirit and intellect.

We easily understand by this figure that man had been emanated only in order to always be in view of the evil demon, in order to contain and combat it.[8]

The power of man was quite superior to that of the demon, since this man joined to his knowledge that of his companion and his intellect, and by these means he would have been able to oppose three good spiritual powers against two weak demoniacal powers, which would have totally subjugated the professors of evil, and consequently destroyed the evil itself.

(*Traité de la Réintégration.*)

"THE TRUE MAN"

You told me that you have not at all been received into the truth by me. I do not know how to have it more certain than that by which I have received you. My state and my quality as true man has kept me in the position where I am. I repeat to you, P.M., that I have for my whole defense nothing but the truth. It is true that I have sometimes imprudently divulged a little too much, and especially to some persons who did not at all deserve it.

THE FALL - MAN DISTINCT FROM HIS BODY

"May 5, 1769.

"I have received the letter that it has pleased you to write me on the date of... of last month. I see with great trouble in my heart the pain and suffering that your nature of material origin has made your body to undergo; but it is of the things with you which are innate and that by these means it is impossible to man and his body to seek the means to operate against the different effects of this first principle. We are born corporeally with seven original evils of which no corporeal form could know and cannot, under any form whatever, avoid; but with a little serious reflection, man is able, however, to weaken and diminish the integrity and the rational and dangerous irritations against the solidity and stability of our personal individuality. Thus, the wise legislators have well foreseen the great inconvenience that man was susceptible to give to his individual by the virtue and authority of his free will, able to consider by it and able to reflect by his relative ignorance on his example and ordinary custom; thus the celebrated spiritual legislator has given seven principal or capital crimes to man, though the seven things be attached to the body and not to man.

LIBERTY OF MAN

Man, alone is responsible to God for the little care and consideration that he has had to have placed indiscreetly in excessive activity the things named above, that I can only explain by the long detail that there would have to be made on it. This, P.M., is the great science of the legislator, as well as the intimate friendship that he has had for man, his equal, and for his spiritual and corporeal preservation that he made seven principal commandments, to which he subjects and constrains the man of desire to follow them scrupulously. These commandments are supported upon the preservation of nature, so that all that would be done by man against nature would be called capital sins. Reflect on this, you will see that there is no enigma at all to what I say when, we being negligent to ourselves, we are negligent directly to God, who is the true father of the creature.

As corollary to this passage, we cite this extract from the *Traité de la Reintegration.*

ORIGIN OF EVIL

"April 8, 1769.

It may be seen by all that I have just said that the origin of evil is not come from any other cause than from the evil thought, followed by the evil will of the spirit against the divine laws, and not that the very spirit emanated from the Creator is directly evil, because the possibility of evil has never existed in the Creator. It is only born from the disposition and will of his creatures.[9]

(*Traité de la Réintégration.*)

THE SECRET SCIENCE

For the other object of which you speak to me, I admit that I would hesitate less to send them to you, if I saw those that you already have in your hands bear more fruit. You do not have the courage, you say, to set to work as much as you do not have the conviction. I tell you that you would be in the greatest error to wait for it on my part; they are absolutely at the disposal of the one who leads us all. The knowledge that I profess is certainly true, because it does not come from man; and the one who exercises it without experiencing the favors thereof must look only to himself. Christ himself has said: "Anything that you ask in my name without hesitating and without wavering in your faith, you will obtain it." That is the true key of the science. I believe therefore to have shown you that the reflections that you make to me ought not stop you. The reason is simple, though you have not any conviction, those that you would admit could have it since there is nothing so free as the march of the spirit, and if you only waited for those convictions in order to build, I would perhaps be able to send you all the materials that I possess, without you valuing them more than the first ones. I do not claim by this to refuse what I have promised you, but I wish that you would make use of what you have.

(November 16, 1771.)

FINAL CONSOLATIONS

Moved by the sentiment and zeal that you have had until the present on behalf of la Chose, it is a guarantee to me that it will not be cruel to you much longer. You must not doubt at all that I am as moved as you are in this regard; but which reassures me that by means of the particular care that I propose to take in order to lead you to this subject, hopefully with the help of L..., I will succeed in putting an end to your punishment.

There is not doubt that your example and your exactitude in the Order that you profess with us, is a striking example for all the members of la Chose. Therefore, I think that although you be on the one hand the last among your brothers and your equals, you become the first with a true resignation and an obstinate perseverance.

(August 24, 1772.)

THE JEWEL OF THE ROSE-CROIX OF THE LODGES OF MARTINÈS
(according to the archives of the Order)

THE GREAT SEAL
PLACED AT THE HEAD OF THE LETTER
OF MARTINÈS
FROM JUNE 19, 1767

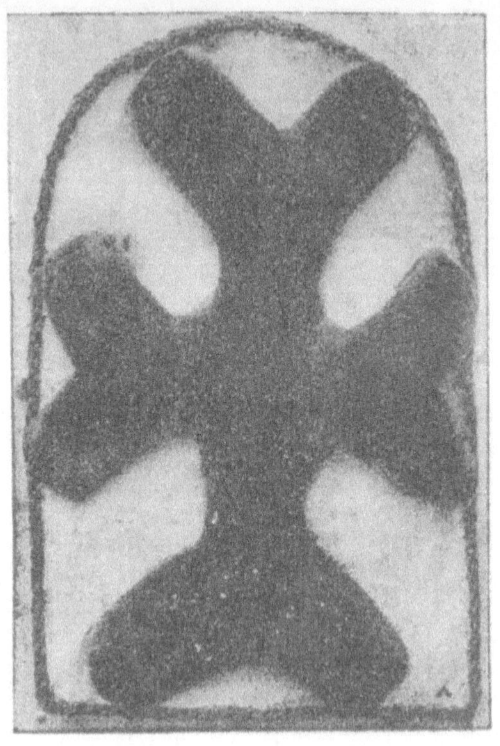

REDCROSS SERVING TO DECORATE THE LODGES
(originating from the archives of Lyon)

D Mr de Pasqually
de Bordeaux 10 9bre 1769

Reception de plusieurs antagonistes
de l'ordre savoir

Mr Duroy d'hauterive
Mr le Baron de Calvimont
Mr de Saignant de Seare Coint
Mr le Cher. de Petrail de Puysegur
les autres &c

Grands succes de Mr de Balzac

SEPARATE SHEET
NOT CORRESPONDING TO ANY LETTER FROM THE ARCHIVES
(writing of Willermoz)

CHAPTER III THE REALIZATION OF THE WORK OF MARTINÈS

THE WORK OF MARTINÈS

We know Martinès de Pasqually under his purely human character, and we have been witness to his tribulations for several years. We have, on the other hand, presented the strange experiences of which Martinès is one of the most glorious representatives. We must now push our investigations even further.

Let us seek how this man, poor on the whole, sustained by his hope in the Truth and his faith in the Invisible, is going to attack a society made gangrenous by the skepticism of the great and by the Pharisaism of the priests; how the initiate is going to create this movement of principal ideas which, passing beyond the revolutionary turbulence, is going to bloom in the middle of the 19th century, in order to bear fruit at the threshold of the twentieth century, still obscure for nearly all!

We are going, first of all, to determine to our best the character of the secret societies considered from the social point of view.

Thus, from there we will understand the aim pursued by Martinès in the constitution of his group of elect Cohens, who are going to struggle everywhere against the materialism of the atheistic lodges, deprived of all tradition.

It is then that we will follow the master into this patient work of realization which did not stop at the tomb, and which still astonishes today the impartial seeker by its majestic grandeur and its great social consequences.

Faithful to our line of conduct, we are first of all going to summarize the most technical points in some pages, and then we will limit ourselves to returning to the analysis of the day to day correspondence.

THE SECRET SOCIETIES AND THEIR ORIGIN

In the human body all the exterior manifestations are the effect of an inner, invisible working. To hold fast only to the verification of the exterior facts is to neglect the part played by the causes; it is running the risk of never foreseeing anything for the future. Likewise, as the bark of the tree is only the result of the interior circulation of the sap, so are many political facts only exterior manifestations of a hidden circulation of the social life.

One of the most active causes of this inner work in action in society is the secret society, true astral body of the manifest society.

The historians take notice, most often, only of the exterior manifestations, of what we may call the bark of society; on the other hand, the conspiracy seekers, the religious writers of this present era especially, see everywhere only the influence of the secret societies. Between these two extremes, the independent seeker ought to be able to make a judicious choice.

The secret society gives rather generally the primordial impulse to the social masses; but these surpass so very often the views of the occult chiefs of the movement, and then are produced these terrible brutal reactions, impossible to foresee.

The duty of the initiates, of those who know how to foresee the social necessities, ought to be making every effort to create men capable of bringing forth useful movements, the evolution of the imperfect forms with a view to realizing the eternal principles in society on the path of evolution.

The summary in some lines of the history of France in modern times will show well this role of the secret societies acting as a true social "astral body."

The current society where parliamentary government has everywhere reached its apogee is only the social manifestation of the organization of the Masonic lodges (since 1773) all constituted according to principles of parliamentary government, of universal suffrage, and of elective tribunals.

Society anterior to the Revolution was only the social manifestation of the religious orders, where the hierarchy held the first place and where submission to the directing Power was the first of the duties.

The Church and the Royalty, in suppressing the Order of the Temple, knew perfectly what they were doing upon the physical plane; but were unaware of what powers they were going to endow the astral plane, source of all realization in the future.

Today the Papacy, feeling its army lost, throws all its soldiers to the assault of the Masonic fortress. But the struggle of these two powers matters little to us; the gnostic spirit, characterized by the alliance of the intuition and science, is henceforth going to vanquish the clerical spirit, and may signify to us the length of the agony of the last vestiges of the Roman She-wolf.

But let us not leave Martinès, nor forget that we are in the era of the preparation of the Revolution, and we see the state of the secret societies in this epoch and the rapid history of their origins.

On the State of the Secret Societies

In the era of the Revolution

We will make our best efforts in the following account to avoid as much as possible the extremes, and, without entering into the very fact of the Revolution, we will study:

1. The state of the secret Societies at the start of the Revolution;
2. The brief history, beliefs, and tendencies of each of these secret Societies;
3. The transformations undergone by these secret Societies immediately before the Revolution.

STATE OF THE SECRET SOCIETIES IN 1785

In 1785 existed three great secret associations united in appearance under the veil of Freemasonry, but each having a most particular spirit and tendencies.

1. *The Grand Orient of France*, constituted since 1772 by the fusion of several Masonic centers whose history we will see further on.

The spirit of the Grand Orient is clearly democratic (but not demagogic). The aim pursued is above all the creation, in society, of the representative régime practiced in the Lodges. The war on clericalism is not yet pursued, at least in the lodges, since among the 629 active lodges that the Grand Orient included in 1789, we find 33 members of the clergy, of which are 27 Venerables (5 at Paris and 22 in the provinces) and 6 deputies to the Grand Orient among the high dignitaries.[10]

The Grand Orient is, therefore, as regards numbers, the most important power.

2. The Grand Chapter General in France, formed by the fusion of the Council of Emperors of the East and West and the Knights of the East.

The Spirit of the Grand Chapter is revolutionary, but the Revolution ought to be accomplished especially to the benefit of the upper middle-class with the people as instrument.

The Grand Chapter, constituted under the régime of the high grades, is issued from the Templar rite, that is to say that the most eminent members are animated by the desire to avenge Jacobus Burgundus Molay and his assassinated companions who have been victims of two tyrannical powers: the Royalty and the Papacy.

The members of the Chapter are less numerous, but, in general, much more instructed, and much more disciplined than the members of the Grand Orient.

It is in confusing the Societies issued from the Templar rite (of Ramsay) with the following, that the majority of historians commit gross errors.

3. *Martinist Lodges*, created by Martinès de Pasqually, and whose center is at this moment at Lyon, directed by Willermoz.

The spirit of Martinism is aristocratic. All is subordinate to the intelligence, and the research pursued bears almost solely on high philosophy and the occult sciences.

The Martinists are very particular in the choice of their members, and the preparatory works are long and dry. They are therefore occupied very little with politics; but, on the other hand, would have a very great influence on the intellectual direction of the Masonic works.

It is under the inspiration of the Martinists that, in the year with which we are occupied (1785), two scientific convents or congresses come to be held which were of a great importance later on: the Convent of the Gaules in 1778, and the Convent of Wilhemsbad in 1782. These gatherings were of truly academic foundations where the highest questions were discussed.

Needless to say, several individuals were part of two of these great associations, or even, like Willermoz, three.

Such are the three great groups whose genesis we are now going to study. We have neglected in this synthetic account, the sects derived from these great sources. We will speak thereof in the course of our work.

THE GRAND ORIENT AND ITS ORIGINS

The Grand Orient of France has issued from an insurrection of certain members against the traditional constitutions and hierarchy of Freemasonry. Some lines of explanation are necessary here.

Freemasonry was first established in England by men already belonging to one of the powerful secret fraternities of the

Occident: the confraternity of the Rose-Croix. These men, and especially Ashmole, had the idea to create a center of propaganda where could be formed unknown to them some instructed members for the Rose-Croix. Thus, the first Masonic lodges were mixed and composed partly of actual workers, partly of workers of intelligence (free masons). The first attempts (Ashmole) date from 1646; but it is only in 1717 that the Grand Lodge of London is constituted. It is this lodge which gives regular charters to the French lodges of Dunkerque (1721), Paris (1725), Bordeaux (1732), etc., etc.

The lodges of Paris multiply rapidly, and name a Grand Master for France, the Duc d'Antin (1738-1743), under whose influence was undertaken the publication of the Encyclopedia, as we will see shortly. Here is the actual origin of the revolution, accomplished first on the intellectual plane before passing from power into action.

In 1743, the Comte de Clermont succeeded the Duc d'Antin as Grand Master of the English Grand Lodge of France. This Comte de Clermont, too indolent to be seriously occupied with this society, named as his substitute a dance instructor, Lacorne, a most intriguing individual, but of deplorable morals. This Lacorne brought into the lodges a mass of individuals of every kind, which led to a scission between the lodge constituted by Lacorne (Lacorne Grand Lodge) and the old members who formed the Grand Lodge of France (1756).

After an attempt at reconciliation between the two rival factions (1758), the scandal became so great that the police became involved and closed the lodges of Paris.

Lacorne and his adherents look to profit from this repose and obtain the support of the Duc de Luxembourg (June 15, 1731).[11] Strengthened by this support, they succeed in returning to the Grand Lodge from where they were banished, had a control commission named whose members were acquired by them in advance. At the same time, the brothers of the Templar rite (Council of Emperors) met in secret on the plots of the commissioners, and on December 24, 1772, a veritable Masonic coup d'Etat is accomplished by the suppression of the immovability of the presidents of the Lodges and by the establishment of the representative régime. Some of the victorious rebels thus founded the Grand Orient of France.

Thus, a contemporary Mason has been able to write: "It is not excessive to say that the Masonic revolution of 1773 was the preamble and harbinger of the Revolution of 1789."[12]

What must be noted well, is the secret action of the brethren of the Templar rite. It is they who are the true fomenters of the revolutions, the others are only docile agents.

Thus, the reader may now understand our assertion: The Grand Orient has issued from an insurrection.

Let us return to two points:

1. The Encyclopedia (intellectual revolution);
2. The History of the Grand Orient from 1773 to 1789.

THE ENCYCLOPEDIA

We have said that the facts to which the historians are especially attached are most often only consequences of occult actions. Now, we think that the Revolution would not have been possible if such considerable efforts had not previously been made to orient the intellectuality of France in a new path. It is in acting on the cultivated spirits, creators of opinion, that one prepares the social evolution, and we are now going to find a peremptory proof of this fact.

On June 25, 1740, the Duc d'Antin, Grand Master of Freemasonry for France, delivered an important discourse in which was announced the great project in progress; witness the following extract:

"All the Grand Masters in Germany, in England, in Italy, and elsewhere, exhort all the scholars and all the artisans of the confraternity to unite in order to furnish the materials for a universal dictionary of the liberal arts and useful sciences, theology and politics alone excepted. They have already begun the work at London; and by the meetings of colleagues, they will be able to bring it to its perfection in a few years.

June 24, 1740

Discourse of the Duc d'Antin

Messrs. Amiable and Colfavru in their study on Freemasonry in the 18th century have grasped perfectly the importance of this project since, after having spoken on the *English Cyclopedia* of Chambers (London, 1728), they add: "To an otherwise prodigious work published in France consisting of 28 volumes in-folio, of which 17 are of text and 11 plates, are then added five supplementary volumes, a work whose principal author was Diderot, seconded by a whole pleiade of elite writers. But it did not suffice him to have collaborators to lead his work to a good end; he had to have powerful protectors. How would he have had them without Freemasonry?

Moreover, the dates here are demonstrative. The Duc d'Antin pronounced his discourse in 1740. We know that from 1741 Diderot prepared his great undertaking. The privilege indispensable to the publication was obtained in 1745. The first volume of the Encyclopedia appeared in 1751.

Thus, the revolution manifested itself already in two stages:

1. *Intellectual revolution* by the publication of the encyclopedia due to French Freemasonry under the great impetus of the Duc d'Antin (1740).
2. *Occult revolution* in the lodges, due in great part to the members of the Templar rite, and executed by a group of expelled Freemasons, then pardoned (Lacorne group); foundation of the Grand Orient under the great impetus of the Duc de Luxembourg (1773) and presidency of the Duc de Chartres.

The Revolution manifests in the Society, that is to say the application to the Society of the constitutions of the Lodges is not going to delay.

Let us return to the history of the Grand Orient at the point where we left off.

Once constituted, the new Masonic power called on all the Lodges to ratify the nomination as Grand Master the Duc de Chartres. At the same time (1774), the Grand Orient was installed in the old noviciate of the Jesuits, Pot-de-fer street, and proceeded to the expulsion of the scabby sheep. 104 lodges first united with the new order of things, then 195 (1776), and finally, in 1789, there were 629 Lodges.

But one fact, to our considerable notice, was produced in 1786. The Chapters of the Templar rite were officially allied to the Grand Orient and had even carried out their fusion with it. We have seen how the brothers of this rite had aided in the revolt from where has issued the Grand Orient; let us, therefore, briefly summarize the history of the Templar rite.

THE TEMPLAR RITE

Freemasonry, we have seen, had been established in England by some members of the Fraternity of the Rose-Croix desirous of constituting a center of propaganda and recruitment for their Order. English Freemasonry knows only three degrees: Apprentice, Companion, Master. By this example, French Freemasonry and the Grand Orient, which was the principal emanation therefrom, were formed by members pursuing only these three degrees. But soon certain men would claim to have received a superior initiation, conforming more to the mysteries of the fraternity of the Rose-Croix, and rites were created to confer degrees superior to that of Master, called *high grades.*

The Spirit of the rites in superior degrees thus created were, of course, different from that of Masonry proper. It is thus that Ramsay had instituted in 1728 the *Système écossais* [Scottish System] whose basis was political and whose teachings tended to make of each brother an avenger of the Order of the Temple. It is from this that we have given the name of *Templar rite* to this creation of Ramsay. The assemblies of the brethren furnished with high grades took the name, no longer of Lodges, but rather of Chapters. The principal Chapters established in France were:

1. *The Chapter of Clermont* (Paris 1752) from where came the Baron de Hundt, creator of high German Masonry or Illuminism;
2. After the Chapter of Clermont appeared the Council of Emperors of the East and West (Paris 1758) from which certain members separated from their brothers forming:
3. The Knights of the East (Paris 1763); each of these powers delivered lodge charters, and the principal brothers (Tschoudy, Boileau, etc.) even create special rites in the Provinces.

In 1782, the Council of Emperors and the Knights of the East unite to form the Grand Chapter General of France, whose principal members had aided in the constitution of the Grand Orient by their intrigues.

We also see, in 1786, these brothers bring about the fusion of the Grand Chapter General of France. What resulted from this fusion?

The members of the Grand Chapter, all quite disciplined, all pursuing a precise aim and possessing *intelligence*, were found to dispose *of the number* furnished by the Grand Orient. - One now understands the Masonic genesis of the French Revolution.

The majority of historians confuse these members of the Templar rite, true inspirers of the Revolution[13], with the Martinists of whom we must now speak.

MARTINISM

In 1754, Martinès de Pasqually, initiated into the mysteries of the Rose-Croix, had established at Paris a center of *Illuminism*. The recruitment of brothers was very meticulous, and the works pursued dealt with the study of ceremonial magic, the ritual of the evocation of spirits, and the absolute dominion of man over his passions and his instincts.

Among the most celebrated disciples of Martinès we will cite the Prince de Luzignan, Louis-Claude de Saint-Martin (the Philosophe Inconnu), and Jean-Baptiste Willermoz, great merchant of Lyon, the true realizer of the Order.

Martinism spread rapidly in France, and, from 1767, many lodges of the west requested affiliation to this rite, just as the correspondence of Martinès that we now publish bears witness.

The Martinist groups and the centers of study derived from Martinism have always left politics aside in order to occupy themselves only with scientific study. It is to these groups that we owe the gatherings or convents which made the greatest steps in the Masonic science. - Thus, the *Philalèthes* (1773), the *Illuminati of Avignon*, the *Academy of True Masons* of Montpellier (1773) derive directly from Martinism.

Here is, moreover, the march of the Masonic rites into Lyon.

In 1752 is founded the Lodge *Parfaite Amitié* according to the ordinary Masonic constitutions. In 1756 this lodge obtains the confirmation of its charter by the Grand Lodge of France. Willermoz is Venerable of this lodge from 1752 to 1763, that is to say for ten years. But, in 1760, the brothers furnished with the degree of Master founded a *Grand Lodge of Masters of Lyon* of which Willermoz was likewise the Grand Master, presiding until 1763.

In 1765 was established a Chapter formed of brothers endowed with the high grades: *Chapter of the Knights of the Black Eagle*. It was the brother of Willermoz, Jacques, medical doctor, who was placed at the head of this Chapter.

In 1767 the Martinist rite was introduced at Lyon and its members were recruited solely among the brethren endowed with the highest degrees, which indicates the value of this Martinist rite.

THE SECRET SOCIETIES OF LYON (1772)

In 1772, here are what were the great Masonic powers represented at Lyon:

1. *The Grand Lodge of Masters* representing the French Rite and presided over by the brother Sellonf;
2. *The Chapter of the Knights of the Black Eagle* representing the Templar Rite and presided over by Jacques Willermoz, physician;
3. *The Élus Coëns* representing the Martinist Rite and presided over by Jean-Baptiste Willermoz himself;
4. Sellonf, Jacques Willermoz, and Jean-Baptiste Willermoz formed a *secret council* having the upper hand over all the centers of Lyon.

It is at the instigation of Jean Willermoz that two great convents were held: *The Convent of the Gaules* (1768) and the *Convent of Wilhemsbad* (1782).

It results from the letters of Martinès de Pasqually that the Martinists, far from supporting the brothers of the Templar Rite in their political projects, fought them to the contrary, always and with all their might. The contemporaries themselves refute the slanders enunciated to this purpose. Bear witness to the following extract:

"The sect of Martinist Freemasons had its center in the *Loge de la Bienfaisance* at Lyon. This lodge deserved the name that it had chosen, by the abundant relief that it gave to the poor. Mr. Robinson has said that its members and their correspondents were impious and rebels. I have known many Martinists, either of Lyon or from various towns of the southern provinces. Far from appearing attached to the opinions of the modern philosophers, they profess to scorn their principles. Their imagination exalted by the obscurity of the writings of their patriarch, disposed them to every kind of credulity; though several were distinguished by talents and knowledge, they had a spirit ceaselessly occupied with revenants and wonders. They were not at all limited to following the precepts of the dominant religion; but they gave themselves to the devotional practices in use among the least instructed classes. In general, their morals were very regular. One noticed a great change in the conduct of those who, before adopting the opinions of the Martinists, had lived in idleness and pleasure seeking. Mr. Barruel maintains that the Freemasons of this sect are *idealists*, that is to say that they do not admit the existence of bodies. This absurd system was never approved but by some pious enthusiasts; but he attributed it to them in order to be able to accuse them of believing that one could never render oneself criminal by the senses, and of approving of prostitution. I do not hesitate to declare solemnly that this assertion is a slander, whose falsehood is demonstrated to me by the most certain proofs."[14]

GRAND ORIENT AND ILLUMINISM

Thus, the Martinists expressed their aspirations in a domain more elevated than that of political struggles.

From 1786, the Martinists, allied with the Illuminati of Baron de Hundt, remain alone in the face of the Grand Orient fused with the Templar Rite. The Revolution was also particularly cruel for the disciples of Martinès - But let us not depart from our subject.

We have wished to show what the respective situation was for the various secret Societies and Freemasonic forces around the year 1789. If we summarize what preceded, we find:

1. On the one hand the Grand Orient (French Rite), into which is fused the Grand Chapter (Templar Rite), possessing nearly all the lodges of the kingdom. The tendencies of these centers are purely revolutionary.
2. On the other hand, the Martinists with purely scientific tendencies, often passing for lunatics, but despising politics. Some lodges of Paris, Bordeaux, and Lyon practiced the Martinist Rite, wide spread by contrast in Germany and Italy.

But we cannot emphasize enough the fact that the majority of authors have confused the brothers of the Templar Rite with the Martinists. These are the leaders who acted with the most violence, and their lieutenants entirely supported the cruel reactions of the crowd.

Once again, we have not had the pretention to remake the history of this period; but only to elucidate a point that many historians have until the present left in the shadows.

The goal of Martinès is therefore in short much less political than theurgical. He wants before all to see to the certain *regeneration of men*, after which, that men know how to properly use their will.

The rite of the Élus Cohen included, as the letter of June 16, 1760, tells us, eight degrees:

Apprentice.

Companion.

Particular Master.

Grand Master Élu.

Apprentice Cohen.

Companion Cohen.

Master Cohen.

To these degrees Ragon (Orthodoxie Maç.) adds a ninth entitled *Knight Commander*.

Some clarification seems to us necessary to this effect.

One will see that in many of his letters, Martinès speaks of the grade of Rose-Croix which one generally obtains only after having had several visions of spirits, duly verified at the time of the great magical operations to which the members of the Order gave themselves several times a year. The title of R.+ seems special and rather independent of the degrees of the Élus Cohens. Is it not to this title that Ragon has wished to allude in his ninth degree?

Alongside the priests of the various religions, Martinès thought, therefore, to constitute some "*groups of elect*" always in communication with the invisible world and being able, consequently, to take the name of true priests or *cohens*.

We are going to see what hierarchy the establishment of these groups possessed, and how they are ruled by a Sovereign Tribunal under the high direction of Martinès (Grand Sovereign). These are the points that the following is going to permit us to better bring into the light of day.

PERSONAL PROPAGANDA OF MARTINÈS

The letter of June 19, 1767, is devoted to the account of the mission of Martinès in the midst of the lodges that he had encountered on his route, at the time of his journey from Paris to Bordeaux.

The Sovereign Tribunal of Paris was constituted at this moment and it is to it that the master addressed the requests for affiliation.

Here is, moreover, the analysis of this important letter of which we reproduce the seal and signatures.

FROM THE GRAND ORIENT OF ORIENTS OF BORDEAUX TO THE GRAND ORIENT OF LYON

June 19, 1767.
In the name of the Great Architect
of the Universe, amen+ amen+
amen+ joy, peace, and prosperity.

"From the Grand Orient of Orients of the Knight Masons, Élus Coëns of the Universe, the Masonic year 3.3.3.3.5.7.9.4.4.6.601, of the rebirth of the virtues 2448, of the world 45, of the Hebraic era 5727, of Christ 1767, of the last in the first quarter of the fifth and sixth moon of the aforesaid year, June 19."

TO THE GRAND ORIENT OF LYON

"To our Very Respectable and Very High Master, our Inspector General, Knight, Conductor, and Commander in chief of the columns of the Orient and Occident of our sublime Orders."

Salutations:
Very Respectable Master be blessed
+
for ever+ o +
+
Amen.

The public and secret conventions that I have taken with my tribunal oblige me to write you and to inform you as a member of all the circumstances which are presented to me in the different towns where I have passed during my route from Paris to La Rochelle, and from there to Bordeaux. I will not give you any circumstantial detail, but a rough sketch, lest it bore you by the multitude of accounts and compliments that I have received on the part of several Masons of good faith, from the various clandestine lodges of all the provinces surrounding Paris, from Ambois, Blois, Tours, Poitiers, La Rochelle, Rochefort, Saintes, Blaye, and Bordeaux.

They also asked me if I would place them under the protection of the Sovereign Tribunal of the Élus Coëns of paris, and if I would see them obtain constitutions, either from it or from me.

I have consequently rewarded the works of brother Basset by conferring upon him the degree of M.·. Élu with the fifth receptacle and to three other brothers of the same lodge that of the Petit Élu with a sole receptable in order to give them the facility to present themselves to the Sovereign Tribunal to request of it constitutions, having left to my Sovereign Tribunal the power to give all sorts of constitutions, wanting absolutely nothing to do with this subject as I have promised and promise to keep with just reason, having almost always been the dupe of my good heart and my too great eagerness, as you may see assured by a number of honest persons when you were at Paris and as you have been able to judge for yourselves.

The M∴. Basset, Venerable of the lodge called l'Union Parfait of La Rochelle, departed consequently last Monday to return to Paris with four of his brothers in order to go present his request to the Sovereign Tribunal.

I am responding to these beautiful discourses, to vanquish without peril one triumphs without glory, and following the maxim of my predecessors, I have my victory consist only in the forgiveness of the guilty which I have done and will do always in similar cases.

Here, Very Respectable Master, is the history of my journey and my conduct at Bordeaux.

Be careful with your power and authority dear Master, do not admit as many as you are able into the knowledge of our mysteries, but those of whom you know to have true zeal as require our general statutes. That is the sole means to shelter the sublime science, which is contained within our Order, hidden under the veil of Masonry."

Your very affectionate and faithful brother
and Master, Don Martinès de Pasqually
G. Sovereign. +
\+ +
\+

FORMALITY FOR THE CORRESPONDENCE

The title to address a letter or a package to the S.T. all together it is necessary to put at the beginning of the first page as follows:

In the name of the Great Architect of the Universe. Amen, then:

Joy, Peace, Salvation.

From the Grand Orient of Orients of Lyon, the Masonic year 3.3.3.-3.5.7.9.- 601, of the rebirth of the virtues 2448, of the Hebraic era 5727, of Christ, commonly styled 1767 from the last and first quarter of the moon (when it is at the end of the Moon to its last quarter). And when the first quarter has begun one puts: From the first and second quarter of the number of the moons which are passed in the antecedent months. Being at the last quarter of this moon, I say: From the last and first quarter of the ninth month September. When one is well acquainted one does not put the month at all. Then one puts the titles of the S.T. as follows: *To the Grand Orient of Orients of the S.T. of the Knight Masons Élus Coëns of the Universe, raised to the glory of the Eternal in the northern region under the Very High and Very Powerful constitutions of our Very Respectable, Very High, and Very Powerful Grand Sovereign, sitting presently at the Grand Orient of Orients, Paris.*

Then one puts at two lines distance:

Very High, Very Respectable, and Very Powerful Sovereign Grand Tribunal,

Then you put what you have to say at four fingers distance. At the end you salute by all the mysterious numbers known only to you, *praying the Eternal that he hold the Sovereign Tribunal in his holy keep, as well as the chiefs in particular who comprise it for a time immemorial; amen, amen, amen.* You sign your ordinary name and all your Masonic qualities or the degree to which you have been most elevated.

If you write to a Rose+ in particular, you put:

In the name O.T.G.A.O.T.U. amen.

Joy, Peace, Salvation.

Then you put:

From the Grand Orient of Lyon.

Considering that you are not writing the body, the Masonic year 3.3.3.3.5. 7.5.7.9.601, of the rebirth of the virtues 2448. You will continue as it says in the other part; after you put:

Very High, Very Respectable, and Very Powerful Master.

Then you say what you want to say. Here, Respectable Master, is what you ask of me.

I have been notified of the reception of the dear brother d'Epernon to whom I wish every kind of success and blessings in all his undertakings. June 20, 1768.

TITLES OF WILLERMOZ

To our V.H., V.R., and V. Powerful Master de Willermoz, Inspector General born of the Universal Order of the Knight Masons Élus Coëns of the Universe, Sovereign Judge of the seven powerful tribunals of justice from the lowest to the highest classes of our Orders, Commander, and Conductor in chief of the columns of the East and West of our Grand Mother-Lodge of France, suffragan and Particular Lodge which will be elevated by him to the glory of the Eternal under the Very Powerful constitutions. From our seventh V.R. and V. Powerful, Chief of the entire Order over his Grand Orient of Lyon and over his oriental department.

IRREGULARITY IN THE RITUAL OF RECEPTION

June 20, 1768.

Some satisfactions that I have had to learn from you and the P. Master Universal Substitute, good acquisition that the Order made in you, the same as with respect to the V. Respectable

Masters d'Epernon and Sellon of your Orient, I am still no less with broken heart at the horrible irregularities which were held during the course of these various receptions by the V.P. Master Du Guers R.+. I am unaware of the motive that has made him act in this way.

THE INITIATES SINCE 1761

Here are the names of the old brothers that I had in my Particular Temple since 1761, who have united themselves with me in order to continue in the science of our Order; the majority are my country neighbors. I will make them members of the Sovereign Tribunal in order to judge and to give their opinions on the affairs that may be reached for or against the good of the Order. Before they sent their opinion from here to Paris, wrote at the bottom of the requests that the V.B. Br. will have to stay here.

Messrs.
D'Aubenton, commissioner general ord. of the Navy
The comte de Maillal d'Abzac, Chevalier de Saint-Louis
De Case, gentleman
De Bobie, commissioner of the Navy, gentleman
De Jull Tafar, old major of the royal grenadiers, Chevalier de Saint-Louis
The Marquis de Lescourt, captain of the Regiment du Roi

I inform you, V.P. Master, that the son that God has given me has been received Grand Master Coëns on last Sunday after his baptism at the seventh hour of the last solar horizon, conforming to our laws, assisted by four of my old simple Coëns named above.

ON THE DEGREE PAPERS

June 20, 1768.

Take care to verify the degrees that he (du Guers) has sent you in order to perform your receptions at your Orient, and if they do not conform to the originals that I have given to the P. Master Substitute, send them to the substitute so that he can send you those conforming to the originals. I do not wish there to be anything composite or apocryphal in any degree of reception; it is necessary to avoid having the confidence and good faith of the men of desire deceived any further, just as they have been by a troop of swindlers, the so-called heads of the Lodge of Clermont. You must judge this by the terrible events that these men have related to us, by their contemptible and evil living and morals, as much in the mental as in the written.

I inform you, V.P Master, that I will not adopt any writing which will be given, whether on the part of the Sovereign T. of France, or from one of my Rose+ to any Grand or Mother Lodge of France, suffragan Temple, or simple Lodge under the pretext of instruction, such as for the ceremonies of reception of the various degrees and classes of the Order, unless it be in order by my Universal Substitute, signed by him and by his Inspector General, his Secretary General, or by the Secretary of the Secret, and that it be signed by my seal. All that will not be signed by it will be regarded by my secret tribunal as clandestine and refused by me as false and thus deprived of my analogous instructions to the Order of legitimate Élus Coëns Masons.

Consequently, I am going to notify by my seal which will be placed at the bottom of each written page which will be given either by me or my Sovereign Tribunal to my Universal Substitute, in order to make use of it according to what will be ordered of him.

April 15, 1768.

I inform you that M. de Saint-Martin wrote me that he is to spend his winter quarter here, perhaps with the R.P. Master de Grainville. I likewise await the V.P. Master de Balzac, who is to come down from La Rochelle in order to stay some days with me for their instruction, - and in order to receive their constitutive patents to raise Temples in the lands where they will be passing through at the end of September or at the beginning of October.

ORGANIZATION AT LYON

September 2, 1768.

Concerning the instructions that you requested of me for the establishment of your Grand Temple of France at Lyon, you may write to the V.P. Master Substitute, whom I am notifying to start sending you the heads of the Temples of our affiliation.

I inform you also that the V.P. Masters d'Aubentons, pay commissioner, and his brother, captain of the upper bank, Chevalier de Saint-Louis, are prepared to be admitted to their grade of R.+ this coming equinox. They have been my disciples for ten years; they deserve the rewards of their works.

I have had here M. Roze and two others of our brothers of Versailles.

ON THE DEGREES

September 27, 1768.

The Master Universal Substitute may pass you the degrees that we have already passed to him; but he will not be sent others until he has indicated the reception of the first, with whose little punctuality I am quite agitated; it has been a month since they were sent to him.

ARRIVAL OF SAINT-MARTIN

I inform you of the arrival of de Grainville into Bordeaux with M. de Saint-Martin who comes for personal business. M. de Grainville lodges and eats with me. I await at once the P. Master de Balzac who is at La Rochelle. I suspect that he has just embarked for Bordeaux.

I will tell you that I am determined to no longer write to the P. Master de la Chevalerie considering that I think that his affairs and his health do not permit him the time to respond to my last letters as well as to indicate to me the reception of the first degrees that I have passed to him, just as the general statutes of the ceremonies of the Order. I do not know what to think of all this, but I know to what it amounts to me concerning the confidence that I have placed in him. Try, I pray you, to instruct me on his manner of action towards the Order and towards its members.

November 25, 1768.

You may write to the P. Master de Grainville who remembers you most kindly as well as the Venerable Master Saint-Martin; they await from you news on the P. Master de Champleon. This does not surprise us at all, we know what he means to do; he awaits your news; but he will only have it after the three months ends of which the P. Master de Grainville has promised him; they end on the fifth of next month and we will write him and at that time we will inform you of what he will have told us concerning his absence from Lyon and why he has not returned to Lyon as he had promised.

January 23, 1769.

Du Guers is driven from the Order. (See the whole history in chap. 1.)

THE TEMPLE OF LIBOURNE

February 19, 1769.

I inform you, V.P. Master, that we have received from the Sovereign Tribunal the constitution for the Temple of Libourne. I will apprise them when we will have delivered it to them to notify you of their establishment to have them recognize you with your particular emulators.

P.S. - I am working with the P.M. Substitute to arrange things in a manner that the Order finally takes a consistence. For it is not all done by establishments, they must be given instructions, etc....! Whatever zeal each of us in particular has for the good of the Order, I doubt that any of us are able to instruct anyone. It is absolutely necessary that D.M. go to Paris and that there, under the eyes of the S.T., he work first in a symbolic bond such as is necessary for the satisfaction of everyone, and that this work ends up, he thinks, to the instruction of the new and old R.+. This transplantation of D.M. and his wife cannot be done without advances on the part of the S.T. Don M. owes here about 1200 pounds which must be paid before leaving, otherwise his creditors would make noise and it would remain to the detriment of the Order.

Grainville.

PROPAGANDA OF THE ORDER

I write you with haste on this Tuesday; after the arrival of the courier from Paris, I expect to receive this day the orders of operation that I have given to the P.M. Substitute during his stay at Bordeaux, so that he copies them at Paris and returns them all to me eventually in order to follow my current equinoxes. Not having them at all, I am obliged to suspend my present work.

I am all ready to found every kind of establishment in ceremony, instruction, laws, and secret explanation, whether for the general and particular officers, or for the general and particular instruction of the brethren, as well as for the particular discourses of reception for Apprentices, Companions, and Particular Masters. I am presently with the instructions of Apprentice, Companion, and Master Coën and with the other degrees. I apprise you that I am working to found the establishment of Bordeaux with some president and councilors of our Parliament.

The Lodges here make some movements to want to enter with us; but this would only take place with great circumspection and difficulty.

I will tell you that Mr. Blanquet has fled Bordeaux with the great talent that I know him to not reimburse anyone. They have made him sell his charge. He has been saved with his harlot, they say, at Paris. The truth is but one, it is long to pierce, but it always shows itself, such as it is. This arrangement has brought the error out of our apocryphal lodges.

BLANQUET

August 8, 1769.

I apprise you that Mr. Blanquet and other chiefs of the bull against me and the Order have failed and have bolted from this Orient. Blanquet must be a little exhausted at Paris with his concubine, the Gauntemps woman. And the truth is avenged.

ORGANIZATION OF THE ORDER

January 20, 1770.

I believe you have made part of the arrangements that I have taken with the P.M. Universal Substitute, which is that the Sovereign Tribunal would give the constitutions signed by my seal and that I would be charged with delivering all the ceremonies of reception of the various degrees of the Order, as well as the various catechisms and secret explanations of the questions and answers, which are contained in the said catechisms. Finally, I will give from A to Z, and everyone will be content.

The arrangement that I have made with the V.P. Substitute is because I fear that his domestic affairs are occupying him much, he is not able at all times to devote himself to everything that is suitable for the Order and for the satisfaction of its members.

Finally, V.P. Master, you must go to Paris in the month of April, you risk no harm either to yourself nor to your brothers, in taking a constitution as have done the brothers of the Temple of Libourne, which was in principle only six persons, one of which was not yet received among us.

I inform you that I have taken on a trustworthy secretary, who has copies of my register of all the degrees, in reception, ceremonies, and particular instructions. Finally, he is definitively charged with the general and particular secretariat. This is a brother that I have had close to me for more than a year, very intelligent. He has abandoned everything in order to follow la Chose in all circumstances. He is called brother Fournier, one of the good bourgeois of Bordeaux. His own uncle is prior of the Grand Augustines of Paris. This brother, not being at all extremely rich, when all the writings necessary to lead a Temple are taken from his hands, he is to be presented with some fees so as not to lose his time absolutely, he is very instructed.

If you truly have the intention to desire to raise your Grand Temple, let me know. I will do everything I can for you, there is a good two months of writing to do, without too many diversions, to send you la Chose in order and properly intelligible.

February 16, 1770.

You have been received by a man who had not any right nor power in this regard: the Master Universal Substitute not having himself the right and the ability to transmit the power to make any

R.+, nor to give any supreme degree, except to transmit his power for the degrees of Apprentice through Master Coën and no more.

PRICE OF THE DEGREES

April 16, 1770.

I inform you that on the first day are to be received M. the Marquis de Ségur, cousin of the first-rate chef, and M. the Marquis de Calvimont, uncle of the brother Baron de Calvimont.

I am in agreement with the P.M. Substitute that the Sovereign Tribunal will only give the constitutions and I myself am charged with giving all the ceremonies of the various receptions; my Sovereign Tribunal having neither the time nor the health suitable for giving itself over entirely to this.

All the brothers that I have here have payed, as well as all the brothers of your Orient, for their degrees. They have not protested at all the money which must be given for their constitutions and for their furnishings; they need not fear to place their money with things so useful and advantageous to the man of desire. The price of the constitutions is rising to two gold louis for each degree. Since you are the Grand Mother Lodge as I have granted you the title verbally at Paris, you will have the power to give up to the degree of G. Architect, which makes in all 16 gold louis in counting from the degree of Apprentice, Companion, Particular Master, Grand Master Élu, Apprentice, Companion, Master Coën, and Grand Master Architect.

I am in a position to make extracts from all the ceremonies of reception of the various general and secret explanations. I have a trustworthy secretary who has written for me for almost a year.

It amounts to a fee to the brother Secretary (for the writings of a Grand Temple) of 86 pounds, not wishing to multiply considerably the establishments relative to the difficulty which appears to me to find subjects fitting to be admitted into our Order. I will tell you that I have received yesterday a letter from P. Master de Grainville where he asks of me the power to advance in degree the brother Barbarin who remains at the Orient with P. Master de Grainville, who certifies to me the progress of this brother, assuring me that he sees much and understands. Consequently, I sent him what is necessary to advance him to the degree of Grand Ar.

Try, P. Master, to tell me that intention of the Sovereign T. to know whether it wants to go forward or to retreat into its state of Rose-Croix. I believe it rather proper, certainly in order to lead la Chose, seeing their great occupations and their little health.

March 13, 1770.

P.S. - The name of the Master Cour...lles is called M, de Grivau, old captain of the infantry.

PROGRESS OF THE ORDER

April 7, 1770.

The Order takes here a brilliant color; the lodges of Bordeaux having been able to obtain nothing from me, for their constitution, they have determined to send off seeking constitutions at Dublin, which is useless in France.

I will tell you that last Thursday it was proposed to admit entry into the Temple some brothers that Mr. du Guers had suborned from my Temple. They have declared verbally to the brother de Laborie and other emulators of my Temple the horrors that Mr. Du Guers had told them of me and the errors where he had plunged them as well as the bad traits, what he had done to them, and that they see today clearly that he has abused and deceived them cruelly and that it is a misfortune.

I have ordered to my council that it is not at all in my power to grant them grace, and that it was useless to think so. Let them follow their decree for a time immemorial.

SUMMARY OF A RESPONSE FROM DOM MARTINÈS FROM BORDEAUX

From July 11, 1770 in 12 articles on the propositions made by the RR.+ at Paris in April, 1770

The M.D.M, has not been able to respond sooner to the propositions because of the last illness of his mother-in-law, which has suspended all correspondence with him.

1. He thanks the V.P. for his offers which prove the true zeal that the R.+ have for la Chose; he owed about 3,000 pounds, he has paid off the majority of it, he still owes 1,000 pounds that he hopes to pay by constraining himself for some time, then he will be free of anyone and able to leave Bordeaux without any fear of insulting his creditors to which he would be exposed if he left before being entirely settled.
2. He does not wish to be a burden upon the R.+, and asks nothing more than to rejoin them, but he wants to do it at his own expense, hoping from their part more fervor in the future than in the past.
3. If the R.+ want to walk exactly in the path that he has prescribed to them by his instructions, being at Paris he will sacrifice himself entirely to all that will be suitable for their advantage and success, and will convince them by this that he has instructed them in good faith and will not be limited in this regard to his journey to Paris and even elsewhere where he will be obliged to transport himself in order to instruct his disciples more particularly; but it is necessary that they be determined of good faith to serve only one sole and legitimate master, their state of R.+ not being able to withstand any division.

4. It is not prudent to make many establishments; seeing the great difficulty of finding good subjects disposed to fulfilling the duties that la Chose requires he could not consent without risking to profane it. All that he could do for the establishments projected by the S.T. would be to five ceremonies of reception, catechisms, and allegorical and symbolic instructions until one or two subjects may be disposed towards the true aim of la Chose; but it would result therefrom that the establishments thus formed would wish to be instructed in the truth, which is not at all at the disposal of the S. Trib. and even less at that of the M. It is therefore necessary to limit oneself to going before the S.T. and the Temp. at Versailles.
5. He does not wish to instruct thoroughly of his own authority any R.+ unless they likewise set themselves to the exact observance of the instructions that he has given them. He would desire much to make a second himself, but it is necessary that the R.+ or a particular R.+ who wishes to attain to this instruction give him convincing proofs that he follows and will follow point for point the instruction and regimen of temporal and spiritual life such as will be transmitted to him when he will have received the response of the S.T. and that he engage himself in following them in the greatest exactitude; it is necessary, moreover, that this R.+ have every necessity to labor 7 years consecutively in the circles of the M. and within his person, such as is explained in the little treatise passed on to him by the P.M. Subs.; one may not succeed otherwise.
6. In regards to the secret papers and instructions concerning the Order that the S.T. recommends to him to bring with him in coming to Paris, he responds that he has never transported such effects right and left, unless he leaves the kingdom where he lives; they are

confided in him only as a deposit that he must give to his successor, and contents himself solely to extract from his originals the things that he believes necessary for the subject who merits them; such a request shows the little confidence that the S.T. has in him on what he may know and say concerning la Chose. He adds that his knowledge is not a particular secret, but rather the fruit of a long and difficult labor of the spirit and a total renouncement of every impure thing.

7. As to the request that they make of him to instruct perfectly the R.+, he responds that he is able to dispose them to procure for themselves the perfect conviction, whenever they would wish to place there much of their own; la Chose being more towards them than towards the M., it is necessary that they wish to follow the M. in good faith and observe with precision all that he will prescribe to them on this subject for the spiritual and temporal conduct, in the different prayers of the days of the year, the equinoxes, the solstices, and the abstinences that they must observe during their life and in the course of a working, just as their exactitude to fulfill with precision the promises that they have made in good faith towards the G.A. of the U. in the resignation that they must have to receive indifferently the good and the pains that it pleases the Eternal to send them for the expiation of their sins and a total renouncement of the things of this lower world. He adds that he could not with impunity veil himself before his disciples without seeking to veil himself before the Eternal; all that he could do in this regard would become useless to him. It is likewise with the R.+ who seek to veil themselves before the M. and to serve him in appearance. He has no less knowledge of the prevarication committed, though he does not complain of it; he is content to pity the subject who separates himself from la Chose. All that the

M. can do and say for the advantage of his R.+ comes not directly from him, it is the fruit of the constancy of his works, it is in this that he exhorts the R.+ to follow him.

8. He responds in general to the things requested by the S.T. which is useless for him to think on before its time, not finding even among the R.+ one subject who is able to make any use of what is given in good faith and would only profane la Chose. The P.M. de Grainville himself knows the impossibility that there is to satisfy this request. He counsels the R.+ before showing such ambition under the pretext of seeking to be instructed, to study well the few ceremonies that he has given them, to reflect upon the spiritual conduct that they have kept in the past, and upon that which is necessary to keep of all necessity in the future; they will then see most clearly that la Chose comes from on high and not from the M.; they will be more convinced that the M. is true and that he has been of the best faith with his R.+; they will come to understand that he is only an agent of la Chose; they will know that the one who is elected first among them is not elected by them and by their will, but that he is so by his painful labors, and his election is his reward. He counsels them again to reflect upon the different types, epoch, and sensible and physical advents occurring in the *universal*, *general*, and *particular* nature, to read a little more particularly, which they have not done up to the present, into the different operations of the Christ, who has actually operated in two substances, the one as Man-God is the quality of true Adam operating upon the earth among the material men; the other as divine man operating by the resurrection, operating with all the spiritual men; they will see by this that it must be truly learned to vanquish all his passions and to submit his will to the one to whom the gift is granted to set la Chose in

action and to serve as example to his disciples; they will learn further how important it is to never despise his fellow-man in pride, every man being infinitely beloved by the Creator, and the most elevated in dignity in this lower world often being the smallest before the G.A. Here are the reflections that the M. exhorts his R.+ seriously in order to have them succeed in the aim that they request.

9. As to the good faith that the R.+ request of the M. in their regard; he responds that it has never been withheld from them, that it may even be ascribed to him to have used it too much towards them in taking it upon himself to advance them before the prescribed time, the little success that they have drawn therefrom proving the little usage and understanding they have of la Chose, and it is no surprise that they have not reserved this firmness that he would hope of them when he left them alone at Paris because they have believed that, la Chose coming immediately from him, they have only to solicit him, frighten him, or offer him great pecuniary concessions in order to have his secret; this not being then in his sole power, it is useless to come to him by this route. He does not complain of what he has done at Paris on behalf of his first disciples in taking it upon himself to receive them R.+, he has been forced there and acted in this in good faith with the intention of making himself a shield of spiritual children, and for proof of which he advances that if he had not been guided in this by the principal chief of la Chose, he would have fallen at the center of his assembly all covered with shame and confusion; his imposture would have been recognized by the little success in his work; instead he had the greatest success possible on behalf of the subjects so poorly prepared to attain to a similar physical operation. The M. adds that seeing all the pains and cruel fatigue that he has

experienced and feels still for the works that he has done on behalf of some subjects before their time, that he no longer wishes to take absolutely anything upon himself henceforth, and that he will undertake nothing on this subject unless it be given and taught to him by someone stronger than him, that to this end he falls back upon what he may know to be produced by some particular work, which he has very strongly explained with the P.M. de Grainville when he was with him in Bordeaux, and which he has expressly declared to him that even though he would engage him by means of solicitations to promise him something that he could not count on at all because he does not hold in him any fashion to grant it; which proves very clearly his sincerity and good faith.

10. The M. wished to find a physical means to open his heart to his R.+ so that they may read there his sincere attachment for them and his recognition for the offers that they make him to procure for him a temporal well-being, whether directly for him or for his wife and children relative to his works. The M. responds to the attention and to the good regards that the R.+ are willing to have for him, that it is not in his power to accept such advantageous temporal offers: 1. Not believing to have merited them; 2. He cannot and must not hope for any temporal and spiritual good in this lower world that does not come directly from the Eternal, to whom he has entirely devoted himself, that he feels sufficiently payed and satisfied of his subjects when he is fortunate enough to restore a man into his first principle of spiritual virtue from which he has had the misfortune to be separated.

11. The M. disapproves of the too great zeal of the P.M. de Grainville in what he has done and proposed on his behalf to the R.+. He should have been well aware of what the M. had said and wrote to him on this subject when he was at the Orient of L., having recommended

to him much discretion for la Chsoe, as much towards its chiefs as towards its members; he did not recognize in this undertaking of the M. de Grainville the great prudence that he has recognized in him on past occasions; it is most unfortunate for the M. that the said M. de Grainville is deluded with expectations of any power over the spirit of his wife. He knew her as poorly as her family who are her support and counsel, before whom, with other persons, strangers, she broke the seal in absence of the M. and read aloud the letter that M. de Grainville wrote her in order to persuade her to convince her husband to accept the offers of the S.T. He knows that she is strongly opposed to what her husband professes generally, la Chose, seeing the great vexations that she has had from the bad subjects who have been admitted there. This letter was in truth more insulting than satisfying over all on the part of the M. de Grainville, who only quite recently has just received new effects from the integrity and good faith of the M. She burned this letter in rage and very nearly saw to also burn secretly the most essential things of the Order which are at the country-house. This letter has caused a great rupture between husband and wife; a third party had to mediate. It has been necessary for the M. to promise to not at all respond to the letter from the M. de Grainville which he has been forced to suspend for some time. He will write, nevertheless, in a few days to his R.+, beloved G.V. returning always the justice that is due to his zeal for the Order and the friendship and attachment that he knows of him for the M. He is entirely convinced that if the M. de Grainville had limited himself to writing only to the M. regarding the S.T., all would have been marvelous and he would now be en route to go to Paris. he would even depart from there sooner on foot than by horse for the unique satisfaction of the S.T. But he has been forced by his state of husband and father of a family to deprive himself yet some time from seeing in person his faithful subjects which will be as soon as he is able; the only consolation until that time is to see them in his spirit.

The M. complains also that the R.+ have not accompanied their requests with a sign at the bottom characteristic of their names, with their grades and dignities in la Chose. The M. could very well ignore such representations and requests, and was in the right to not respond at all, the crest at the top not sufficing to obtain it. Those who have conducted similar things have been neglectful to the laws of the Order.

12. The M. exhorts the R.+ to reflect upon the response that he made to their requests and objections; they will see there clearly his sincerity and his good faith. The S.T. would be wrong to think that the M. expresses himself in this way to wish to abandon the Order and its members; he works on the instructions by writing more than ever and is presently occupied with a work which will satisfy not only the just men but will be most fitting to withdraw the greatest scoundrels from their errors and to lead them to be filled with happiness. This work has for its title *The Reintegration and Reconciliation of every created spiritual being with its first Virtues, Strength, and Powers in the personal enjoyment of which every being will enjoy distinctly in the presence of the Creator*; and does not make this work assuredly for himself alone, the things that he knows sufficing for himself. he must think of his faithful subjects whom he will not abandon from his life, provided that they wish to preserve in la Chose and to follow him blindly.

The M. exhorts the R.++++ to pray for the rest of the soul of his mother-in-law, just as she requested before her death.

Nota. - The present response is without other signature.

THE WORK OF MARTINÈS

December 16, 1770.

You will receive in a little while one of my letters which will instruct you in what I have done for the general good of la Chose and its members. It is an immense work; you will judge it by the title of the two folios - you may, if you are pressed to give the degree of Grand A. to the P.M. de la Chevalerie, procure it for yourself from the original that you have in hand. I will eventually make up the deficiency of what will not be complete and will communicate to you the new orders of this degree that he may lack.

Nothing will be operated but the previous; all the members of the Order in general are in order, conforming to the deliberative judgment that I just gave in my circle. This judgment will be sent to you shortly, just as it is sent to the P.M.+ of Foix and to some other members of the Order at a distance from the chief town.

THE ABBÉ ROZIER

April 27, 1771.

M. abbé Rozier has had to write you in order to be admitted among you and me. Respond to him consequently. This is a man full of desire; he does not leave my sight when he can join me; he remains with me until midnight. He begins to be persuaded that it is here that he will find what he has sought for so long. I had him apply for his admission, however I will abbreviate his anxiety according to what you write me and according to what I will find him capable of. M. de la Borie, my second self that I have with me, charges me to speak well to you of things on his part as well as M. Cagnet who is of an astonishing zeal.

November 1, 1771.

I am instructing you again that I have delivered the constitutive patents to my cousin Cagnet. He has left for Port-au-Prince in the capacity of commissioner general of the navy.

The M. de Saint-Martin labors always for you.

M. abbé Rozier has written me in order to make the same complaints to me that you have made to me on this subject. I have responded to him that the degree that he had was that of Grand Élu, that despite all the justice that I cannot refuse him, I have had my reasons for advancing further Miss Chevrier who has actually labored in this line of work for long years; that for the treatise he was still too newly admitted to confide it in him. May he not weary in persevering in confidence and may the light never be able to be removed from him.

Miss de Chevrier is at the degree of M. Coën.

RECEPTION OF NEW MEMBERS

January 13, 1772.

It will not be possible for me, Very Beloved Master, to give you either rule or manner to comport yourself with regard to the subjects that you would desire to lead into the Order. Any instructions that I will send you on the subject will be found disturbed by the least circumstance; that is why the Christ prohibited with such care to his disciples of ever preparing themselves on what they would have to say and this because they had to have confidence that he would always be with them and that they would thus have no more need of anything.

THE INSTRUCTIONS AND THE DEGREES

October 12, 1773.

In la Chose, the praises that the V.P.M. Desère, Universal Substitute D.L. has given me for your exactitude to fulfill scrupulously all your duties in la Chose and towards those who follow you, puts me in the circumstance to leave you nothing more to desire in order to place you in a position to go all alone to the aim that you desire of la Chose that you have embraced. Consequently, I inform you that I have made here all the instructions of the different grades of L.·. from the Class of the Porch up to that of R.+, then the general index of names, numbers, in conjunction with the characters and hieroglyphs, the various tables of operation, and the various invocations which must follow the tables. The general index interprets the fruit arising from the operation. With all these pieces the R.+ may interpret the fruit of their labors without my help. Consequently, I dispose myself to transmit to the V.P.M. Du Roy d'Hauterive, newly ordained by correspondence R.+, some instructions so that he passes them on to you with the consent of the V.P.M. Desère, substitute. I wrote on the subject to the V.P.M. Du Roy and Desère in order to procure for myself more promptly the said instructions, in order that you communicate them to the disciples of your G.T., those that you find most worthy to receive them and especially the Br. Orcel of whom I have been assured makes a great subject for la Chose, whom I hope to promote by the success that he may have in L.

I pray you to embrace him for me as well as your dear sister of whom they have spoken praise to me of the desire that she has to succeed in the aim of la Chose, as I think that you have given her some instructions relative to la Chose and that she has profited well therefrom, I exhort you to cultivate her while waiting for me to be able to send you what is necessary for her reception and the order to receive her, which is here all ready on this subject, having a lady to receive if she is worthy. She is well instructed, but I will act on her behalf very slowly. We must not desire the quantity of subjects; but rather the quality.

The Order here is going pretty well. There are great subjects at the S.T. that the V.P.M. Caignet has established at Port-au-Prince. I hope it is the same for your G.Or.

I exhort you to suspend until new orders the recognition of the V.P.M. de Cressac, last R.+, for reasons known to the S.T. of the G. Or. of this colony, of which you will be instructed later, and may all that may reach you on his part be regarded as void.

THE SUCCESSORS OF MARTINÈS

The V.P.M. Caignet, who is overwhelmed by the weight of the affairs of his position, charges me to tell you a thousand things on his part, the ones more beautiful than the others; being unable to avail himself of the present occasion to write you, having written you without having received any response. Respond to him; as my intention is to leave in deposit all my originals into his hands, for reasons powerful to my knowledge, it is further reason for you to establish your correspondence with him, being obliged to issue from him all the instructions necessary to the Order and its members.

THE NATIONAL LODGE OF FRANCE

April 24, 1774.

I will not hide from you that the P.M. Caignet just as myself, as well as all the members who comprise the G.S.T. of my G.O. have been surprised and even astonished when they have seen your name on a printed package which concerns the National Lodge of France and that solicits a sum of money by virtue of free gift from men of distinction in every respect, from the various lodges of the Kingdom under the pretext of having a Temple constructed for the installation of M. the Duc de Chartre. How to reconcile this conduct of requesting money freely by persons of so high consideration whose personal state announces an infinite wealth and opulence. Is not a similar step taken to surmise that there are some in the know, and that it is a wind-fall of money that they wish to make. It is even scandalous for the persons who expect to see that some persons of name and of the highest consideration, would be party to such a thing, that however they do not believe here. It seems from this printing that M. de la Chevalerie is at the head of this new establishment, and it makes the abbé Rozier an indifferent agent; but he is there for something. The Order with us does not retain any of its subjects by force; on the contrary, it leaves them as it has taken them; they are always free; for otherwise they would not at all merit to do good in preference to evil. Explain to me how your name is found placed in this printing that the P.M. Caignet has received from Paris and a second similar volume that they have addressed to him these past days, which has had the same fate as the first which has been inconsiderable.

The greater part of the lodges which were in this colony are entirely fallen.

There no longer remains in that of Port-au-Prince but some subjects that the general and secret statutes exclude in perpetuity from la Chose, being over all marked with the letter B from birth and among others the bastards and the mixed-bloods.

The letter that I wrote to the P.M. de Saint-Martin is signed by the hieroglyph of the G.S. and by that of the Sovereign Substitute overseas and signed in full by the Secretary General of the said S.T.

THE GENERAL STATUTE

I profit from the departure of F. Timbale, who is going to Bordeaux in order to inform you of the mailing that the S.T. of Port-au-Prince sends you, which consists of the new General Statute that you will follow regularly and will have followed by all your disciples in all it contains. He sends you likewise the catechism of Commander of the Orient, you will receive all of it by way of the V.P.M. Du Roy d'Hauterive. There are still the statutes for the reception of women and the tables for the reception of the first three degrees. You will conform yourselves in this regard, as it is said in the last chapter of the General Statutes that I send you, while waiting for me to inform you of the Secret Statutes that you will receive from the S.T. of Port-au-Prince. I am notifying you that the V.P.M. Sovereign Substitute Caignet writes you by the same way as well to the P.M. de Saint-Martin. His letter is included in your letter. Write to the P.M. d'Hauterive so that he sends you promptly from Bordeaux what I write to you. I inform you that the V.P.M. Caignet de Lester has been made Grand M. R.+ He has right of custom; he has here my presence and my absence. I will send in a short while to your Grand Temple the order of proclamation of the P.M. Caignet so that you can inform all the members of the Order who are in the Grand Orient of France.

P.S. - Read with care the General Statute that I send you certified and sealed with the great crest of the Order. You will take care to have it signed by all the brothers of your G.L. on the pages which remain with the present statute.

THE ADEPTS OF MARTINÈS

We are now going to arrange as best we can a list of the principal personages who have followed the rite of Martinès. We will take care to indicate the date when each person is named for the first time.

Names	Date of the letter when the name is cited for the first time	Observations
Basset	June 19, 1767	
d'Epernon	September 19, 1767	
Sellon	June 20, 1768	

Du Guers	June 20, 1768	Driven from the Order
d'Aubenton	June 20, 1768	
Comte d'Abzac	June 20, 1768	
de Case	June 20, 1768	
de Bobie	June 20, 1768	
de Julli Tafar	June 20, 1768	
Marquis de Lescourt	June 20, 1768	
Claude de Saint-Martin	August 3, 1768	
de Grainville	August 3, 1768	
de Balzac	August 3, 1768	
Willermoz brother (physician)	August 13, 1768	
Brother of M. d'Aubenton	September 2, 1768	
de la Chevallerie	October 2, 1768	Substitute
de Champolion	November 25, 1768	
Lce. & Lien. de Luzignan	February 19, 1769	
Dessingi	August 8, 1769	
Fournier or Defournier	January 20, 1770	
de Hauterive	February 16, 1770	
Desère	February 16, 1770	Captain of the artillery, under-commissary of the artillery of the castle of Bordeaux
Baron de Calvimont; Cabory	February 16, 1770	
Schild	February 16, 1770	
Marcadi	February 16, 1770	
Marquis de Ségur	February 16, 1770	
Marquis de Clavimont	February 16, 1770	
Barbarin	February 16, 1770	
M. de Grivau	March 13, 1770	
Corbis	April 7, 1770	
the abbé Rozier	August 27, 1771	
M. de la Borie	August 27, 1771	
Caignet de Lester	August 27, 1771	Successor of Martines
Miss de Chevrier	November 26, 1771	Maître Coën
Orcel	October 12, 1773	

de Cressac	October 12, 1773	Suspended, stricken from the Order
Timbale	August 3, 1774	

CONCLUSION

THE CRITICS AND MARTINÈS
The role of the Martinists from Martinès to our day.

MARTINÈS AND HIS BIOGRAPHIES

We have the occasion, with respect to Saint-Martin, to return to the numerous errors committed, document errors, by the critics who have occupied themselves with Martinès.

Adolphe Franck, in his work on the Mystical Philosophy in France, is obliged to report, on the very person of Pasqually, the obscurity which surrounds his work, and it is not without a slight smile that the reader, who has just perused the documents that we have brought to the light of day, will read the following extracts drawn from the book of Adolphe Franck:

"For example, what do we know of Martinès Pasqualis, this mysterious personage, come from who-knows-where, that one encounters everywhere and that one may not comprehend any part of, who disappeared as subtly as he came, going to seek far away an end remaining unexplained, like his life, after having exercised upon Saint-Martin a decisive influence?"

"The cloud that enveloped his life is not completely dissipated by the book of Mr. Matter, nor even by the unpublished documents that Mr. Matter has had the generosity to place at my disposal.

"We know that he was the son of a Portuguese Israelite, who has come, one knows not at what date or for what reason, to be established at Grenoble.

"I cannot, therefore, share in the common opinion that makes of Martinès Pasqualis an Israelite converted to Catholicism:

one has never cited a single fact which demonstrates this pretended conversion. He has never pronounced nor written a single word that one may interpret as a profession of Catholic faith."

Now, we have seen that Martinès possessed his certificate of Catholicity, that he followed the religious offices, and that he had his son baptized.

That is for the religion.

As to the origin of his family, we are obliged to remain in doubt until the day when we find the copy of the marriage certificate of Martinès, that we have sought in vain up until now. Let us adopt till further orders the date of 1715, given by Ad. Franck for the birth of the master; but we absolutely reject the Israelite origin and are prudent on the question of his Portuguese ancestry.

The author of the biography of Martinès in the "Michaud" dictionary says with reason: "Even the most intimate disciples of Martinès have not known his homeland. It is according to his language that they have presumed that he could be Portuguese and Jewish."

Adolphe Franck, always very scrupulous when it is a question of setting a date, admits for the birth of Martinès the year 1715. - "Born around 1715 in Portugal or at Grenoble to a family of Portuguese Israelites."

STATE OF MARTINISM FROM ITS FOUNDATION TO OUR DAY

What has become of the work of Martinès?

The letters of Saint-Martin and Willermoz give us all the information necessary on this point.

It is Willermoz who, alone, after the Revolution, continued the work of his initiator, by amalgamating the rite of Élus Cohens with the Illuminism of Baron de Hundt in order to form the *eclectic Rite.*

Certain degrees of this rite were purely Martinist, just as we learn of the organization instituted at Lyon (see the *State of the Secret Societies at Lyon in 1772*, chap. III).

M.J. Mounier, in his work on the *Influence attributed to the Freemasons in the French Revolution*, says to have known many Martinists spread throughout the towns of the southern provinces.

Finally, the following passage from a letter of Willermoz allows us to follow with certitude the Martinist Order until 1810: "I just spoke of a Masonic Establishment formed at Paris in 1808 and that I have then constituted likewise in provisional prefecture. There are many prospering there under the title of *Loge du centre des Amis*. It is a nursery of the Order which has already rendered us great services. For it is by the cares of the principal members of this lodge, who were deputies with me at Lyon to obtain and copy the rituals, instructions, and documents of all the degrees of the Régime, that we owe the honor and the inappreciable advantage to now have a chief, a protector, and a national Grand Master of the Rectified Régime in France, in the person of Sér., brother of Cambacérès (in ordine Eques Joanes Jacobus Regis a legibus)."

(*Letter from Willermoz to Prince Charles de Hesse-Cassel*)

The following passage indicates further that the Order had made serious progress at Libourne:

"In an initiation, the Br.·. Jean Mathieu, age twenty-three, merchant at Libourne, was called to abjure the errors which have been raised against him in a false Lodge generally condemned and notably by the V.·.R.·.G.·.L.·. of F.·., which errors were dictated by the profane and disturbing Paschalis and his sect."

(*Hist. de la Fr.-Maconnerie a Angouleme, by Dents Mamoz, 1888, in8vo.*)

From this era until 1887, the Martinist Order was transmitted by groups of initiators spread especially throughout Italy and Germany.

At the date of 1887, a great effort was attempted for the real diffusion of the Order, and four years later (1891), the acquired results permitted the creation of a Supreme Council of twenty-one members, having under its obedience several lodges in France and throughout Europe.

Moreover, a great number of Free Initiators S.·.I.·. assure in a definitive manner the propagation of the Order.

The choice made of our center by the Masters of the Invisible to deposit there the archives of the Order, is a great honor to us that we will strive to justify as best we can in the future.

APPENDIX

The Catechisms of the Élus Coëns

CATECHISM
OF APPRENTICE ÉLU COËN

Q. Are you apprentice Élu Coën?
A. Yes, I am.
Q. How have you been received Apprentice Élu Coën?
A. By submitting to the order of the Master and that of the Temple.
Q. How were you placed when they received you Apprentice Élu Coën?
A. I was neither naked nor clothed, divested of all metals, my body placed at the center of six circumferences, forming a long square and four perfect Squares.
Q. What have you seen in this position and what have you heard?
A. Nothing that the human Spirit may comprehend.
Q. Why is that?
A. Because I was deprived of the use of my corporeal and spiritual senses.
Q. What did you see when you received use of your senses?
A. A vast light, a great frightful commotion, and three great columns.
Q. What have you observed on the three great columns?
A. Three hieroglyphs which were placed separately in the form of a triangle on each.
Q. What did these three hieroglyphs represent to you?
A. The three different spiritous essences which compose the general, terrestrial, celestial, and particular body.
Q. How will you attain to the perfect knowledge contained within the Order and how will you develop the hieroglyphic characters which are marked on each of the said columns?
A. By forcing myself to labor with zeal and without relaxing to the general good of the Order, by which means I will attract to myself the benevolence of the chiefs who will unite their works with mine, in order to see me succeed in the perfect enjoyment of the

rights, fruits, and prerogatives of the Order by the legitimate spiritual Élus Coëns.

Q. What are the instruments of which the G.A.O.T.U. has made use for the construction of the universal Grand Temple?

A. A triangle, a perpendicular, and a perfect square.

Q. What form has your general temple?

A. A perfect equilateral triangle, just as it is represented to us from north to south, and from south to west.

Q. What is its height?

A. Numberless cubits.

Q. What is its depth?

A. From the surface to the center.

Q. What is its length?

A. From east to west.

Q. What is its breadth?

A. From north to south.

Q. What covers this vast edifice?

A. A canopy studded with stars.

Q. What are the most useful numbers of which the Apprentice Élu must make use in the Order?

A. 3, 2, 5, 6, 7.

Q. What is the word of the Apprentice Élu?

A. Of seven kinds.

Q. Give them.

A. He gives them.

Q. What is the particular sign of the Apprentice?

A. The right hand resting squared upon the heart, and the left hand squared edge- wise over the ground.

Q. To what alludes the seven signs?

A. S.V.J.M.Mer. Sn. Mn.

Q. At what hour of the day are the three Porches of the Temple opened?

A. At full midday.

Q. At what hour are they closed?

A. At full midnight.

Q. Upon what rests the temple of the Apprentice Élu of the Universe?
A. Upon three powerful columns.
Q. Where are they placed?
A. The first towards the East, the second towards the North, and the third towards the South.
Q. What is their height?
A. Eighteen cubits.
Q. What covers their top?
A. A double capital adorned with pomegranates.
Q. What is their circumference?
A. Twelve cubits.
Q. Were the columns empty or full?
A. They were empty.
Q. Why is that?
A. In order to contain the powerful instruments used by the G.A.O.T.U. for the construction of his universal temple.
Q. By what will I know that you are at the degree of Apprentice Élu Coën?
A. By my signs, operations, and the circumstances of my reception, that I will give to you faithfully.
Q. How do the Apprentices of our Order travel?
A. From the West to the East, and from the North to the South.
Q. What is that?
A. Because I have not acquired the requisite age that is expected of me according to my works, the zeal for duty to the Order, and the perseverance to practice virtue.
Q. What is the battery of the Apprentice?
A. Three slow strikes.
Q. To what does this battery allude?
A. To the three principles which compose the temporal Temple of the Apprentice.
Q. Name them.
A. M.S.S.

Q. To what part of the body do you apply the first principle, Mercury?
A. To the osseous part.
Q. To what do you apply the second, Sulphur?
A. To the fluid part.
Q. To what do you apply the third, Salt?
A. To the pellicular part.
Q. What does the solid part designate?
A. The general terrestrial body.
Q. What does the fluid designate?
A. The solar part.
Q. What does the pellicular part designate?
A. The northern part.
Q. Have you seen your Master today?
A. Yes, V.R.M.
Q. How is he dressed?
A. White, red, and black.
Q. To what do these three things allude?
A. To beauty, virtue and wisdom.
Q. To whom do you give beauty, virtue and wisdom?
A. Beauty to the work of the Creator, virtue and wisdom to the Apprentice Élu.
Q. What is your age?
A. Three years.
Q. What must an Apprentice observe?
A. Three things: perseverance, temperance, and charity towards all his brothers.
Q. What must he flee?
A. Three things: slander, idleness, and wickedness.
Q. Have you any ornaments in your Temple?
A. There are three therein, which are: the law, the circle, and the triangle.
Q. In what place do the Apprentices work in the Temple?
A. In the northern part.
Q. What is their genre of work?

A. To raise spiritual edifices upon their base according to the plan that they received from their Master.
Q. How many kinds of Temples are there in the universe?
A. Five kinds: the simple, the perfect, the symbolic, the just, and the apocryphal.
Q. What is the simple?
A. It is that of the body of man.
Q. What is the perfect?
A. That of the universal body.
Q. What is the symbolic?
A. That of the general terrestrial body.
Q. What is the just?
A. That of the inferior material body.
Q. What is the apocryphal?
A. It is the conventional one that men are forced to establish with impunity in error.
Q. What is the attribute of an Apprentice?
A. A perpendicular.
Q. What does the perpendicular designate?
A. That all the actions and operations of the Apprentices ought to be directed by the principle of his spiritual emanation.
Q. With what do you serve your Master?
A. With zeal, fervor, and constancy, indicated emblematically by the chalk, the earthenware dish, and the charcoal.
Q. How long do you serve your Master?
A. From Monday to Saturday.
Q. In what time begins the strength of your work?
A. At full midday and ending at midnight.
Q. What are the conditions of your reception?
A. An authentic promise and inviolable obligations.
Q. With whom have you contracted all these things?
A. With the G.A.O.T.U. in the presence of the R.V.V.M. of the East and West, and all the brothers of the Temple.
Q. What has it cost you to make you Apprentice Élu Coën?

A. My good will and a piece of gold valued above the general and particular statutes of the Order.
Q. Have you any jewels in your Temple?
A. Yes, V.R.M. There are three, which are: the square, the compass, and the tracing board.
Q. Of what use is the square in the Temple?
A. To perfect the works of the Particular Apprentices.
Q. To what serves the compass?
A. To direct and limit those of the Companions.
Q. To what serves the tracing board?
A. It serves to decorate the Particular Masters, and to indicate the superiority of their works in the Class of the Porch.
Q. Why is a moon and a sun traced in the Temple?
A. To teach us to know perfectly the faculty of the elementary fire, and the moon to teach us likewise its property in the act of conception and vegetation.
Q. What are the first elements of the Order of the Apprentice Élus Coëns?
A. The tracing, the operation, and the word.
Q. How have you arrived in the Temple?
A. By ascending seven steps.
Q. Do you know the virtue and the property of these seven steps?
A. No, V.R.M, but it is hoped that I will gain this knowledge for myself by the exactitude of my works, that the principal Masters will reward after the expiation, limited term.
Q. Where stands the R.M.?
A. At the Orient.
Q. Where stands the V. Master?
A. At the Occident.
Q. Why do they stand in these parts?
A. The R.M. stands in the Orient in order to direct all the spiritual actions and operations of the Élus Coëns, and the V. Master stands in the Occident in order to set the workers to labor, to conduct and direct all their material, temporal, and spiritual operations in the general Temple.

Q. Why do they divest a recipient of all metal at the time of his reception?
A. To make allusion to the formation of all the bodies that the G.A.O.T.U. has constructed in the universal Temple without the help of material operation.
Q. Why do they hold a sword at the time of the reception of a candidate?
A. To allude to the one that the G.A. had march against the enemies of his holy law and against those of his elect.
Q. Why are different signs and words given in the L. of the different classes of the Order?
A. In order to distinguish the different workers and to avoid that way that they not be surprised and confused among the profane.
Q. At what age is an Apprentice received into the Order?
A. At the age of twenty-one years completed.
Q. At what age is the son of a Master received in the Order?
A. From sixteen or seventeen years old, having right to five years grace in his capacity of louveteau [lewis].
Q. What is the quality of an Apprentice Élu Coën?
A. To be a free man, equal to Kings and to every man when he is virtuous.
Q. What does the Order of Apprentice Élus Coëns teach to its disciples?
A. To know perfectly the existence of the G.A. of the Universe, the principle of the spiritual emanation of man, and his direct correspondence with his Master.
Q. What is the origin of the Order that we profess?
A. The origin comes from the Creator and begins from the first times under Adam and until our day.
Q. How has this Order been able to be perpetuated unto us?
A. By the pure mercy of the G.A., who has raised by his Spirit subjects proper and suitable to manifest this Order among men for his greater glory and Justice.
Q. Of what usefulness was this Order to the men of the first time?

A. It served them as spiritual basis and foundation in order to operate the ceremonial of the cult of the Eternal and to preserve them that way in the regularity of their first principles, virtues, and divine spiritual powers.
Q. What are the names of the subjects that the G.A. has used in order to perpetuate this Order unto us?
A. From Adam until Noah; from Noah to Melchizedek, to Abraham, Moses, Solomon, Zorobabel, and Christ.
Q. Do you know how to read and write in the Order?
A. No, V.R.M.
Q. Why is that?
A. Because it is forbidden to me and because I have promised by my oath.
Q. What is the limit of the Order of the App. Élus Coëns?
A. There isn't any; it spreads from the four celestial regions, upon the three terrestrial ones, and from there to all the nations of the world.
Q. What are the different conventional words, signs, and grips of the apocryphal Élu Masons?
A. For the Apprentice, Jakin, the password tubalkin; for the Companion, Booz, the password, schibolet; for the Master, Makbenac, the password, Giblim.
Q. What is the sign of the apocryphal Apprentice, and his grip?
A. Hold the right hand squared on the throat, feigning to cut the neck, then let fall said hand upon the right side; the grip is to take the right hand of the one to whom one wishes to give the grip with his right hand, then rest the thumb of said hands upon the first phalanx of the index, and to rest the said thumb three different times, upon said phalanx.
Q. What is the sign and touch of the apocryphal Companion?
A. Hold the right hand in the form of a claw over the heart in order to want to tear it away; for the touch, take the right hand as is said for the Apprentice and rest the thumb upon the first phalanx of the middle finger as done for the Apprentice.
Q. What is the grip of the M. of this Order and the sign?

A. The grip is given by taking the right hand reciprocally in the form of a claw as wishing to tear out the whole palm of the hand; their sign is that of bringing the open right hand in front of the eyes, as if wishing to make a sign of horror or repugnance.
Q. What are the words of the different apocryphal degrees?
A. For the Master Élu, *Nekam* or *Nekoum*; for the Scottish Master, *Neder*, *Bery*, *Jeova*; for the Master Architect, *Jeova*, *Salomon*, *Accasia*; for the Knight of the East, *Zorobabel*, *Judas*, *Binjamin*; for the Knight of the Sun or Commander, *Tito*, *Zinsu*, *Ain*, *Salomon*, *Hiram*; for the Rose-Croix, *Inri*, *Jeova*, *Hei*, *Halmie*.
Q. What connection have all these signs, grips, words, and figures of the apocryphal Élu Masons with those of the Élus Coëns?
A. There aren't any.
Q. Why do the apocryphal Masons use some of our signs and emblems in their assemblies?
A. As having penetrated little into the Science and into the profound Mysteries of the Élus Coëns of the Universe, they have formed a Masonic Order at the example of the construction of the Temple of Solomon in which they have found some of our emblems, the virtue, property, and perfection of which they are unaware.
Q. In what book is written the name of the Apprentice Élus Coëns?
A. In the Immemorial book which has neither beginning nor end.

END OF THE CATECHISM OF THE APPRENTICE

CATECHISM
OF COMPANION ÉLU COËN

Q. Are you a Companion Élu Coën?
A. Yes, V.R.M., I am.
Q. How have you been received Companion?
A. By passing from the perpendicular to the triangle.
Q. Why have you come out of one to pass to the other?
A. I have come out of this first principle of my own will, and I travel upon the material triangle until the perfect expiation of my prevarication.
Q. What, then, is this prevarication which has been able to subject you to such a vile and painful journey?
A. The horror of my crime upon the person of the innocent which still requires vengeance to the Eternal of the effusion of his blood.
Q. What is the effusion of this blood which may be offered to the G.A. of the Universe?
A. It is blood superior to that of human nature.
Q. Can you name it?
A. I cannot, not yet being permitted to me in the present circumstance until my perfect reconciliation.
Q. Have you seen your Master?
A. No, Very Venerable.
Q. How can you know him if you have not seen him?
A. It suffices me to admire all his spiritual and temporal works in order to know him perfectly in all his divine spiritual virtues and powers.
Q. How do you serve your Master?
A. By the pain of *body*, *soul*, and *spirit*.
Q. How long do you serve him?
A. From one sunrise to the other.
Q. Why is that.
A. In order to acquire the age of perfection.
Q. What is the number of the ages of perfection?

A. From the number of five, of six, until that of seven.
Q. What does the quinary number explain?
A. My prevarication.
Q. What does the senary number explain?
A. My emancipation.
Q. What does the septenary number explain?
A. My reconciliation.
Q. Are you reconciled?
A. No, V.V., I cannot be at the previous until I have acquired the promised age.
Q. Where is the Temple of the Companions situated?
A. In the area of the South.
Q. Why is it set in this place?
A. Because this is the place that the G.A.O.T.U. has destined to the Companions of prevarication who have had the misfortune to fall prey to the iniquitous instructions and operations of the demon.
Q. What is the sign of the Companion?
A. The right hand squared, raised over the heart.
Q. What is the step of the Companions?
A. It is by three triangular steps.
Q. What is the battery of the Companions?
A. Five strikes, three quick and two slow.
Q. How do the Companions travel?
A. From the West to the North, and from the North to the South.
Q. Where do the Companions stand in our Temple?
A. In the South.
Q. Why is that?
A. In order to designate the frightful dwelling of the first prevaricators against the cult of the Creator.
Q. Upon what do the Companions work?
A. Upon the perfect knowledge of temporal matter.
Q. What are the principal numbers of the Companions?
A. 2, 5, 6.

Q. What does the number two designate?
A. The number of confusion, represented by the two columns of the Porch, which indicate action by that of the North and contraction by that of the South.
Q. What does the number five designate?
A. The degradation of the first Elect man by the demoniacal power.
Q. What does the senary number designate?
A. The origin of my corporeal emanation, represented by the six circumferences of my admission into the Order.
Q. What must a Companion observe in the Temple?
A. To work, to obey, and to keep silence.
Q. What does the sign of the Companion designate?
A. Pride and the crime of his operation.
Q. In what do you know the crime of the prevarication of the Companion?
A. By his spiritual privation, represented by his corporeal prison.
Q. What is the attribute of a Companion in the Order?
A. It is none other than that which has procured for him his prevarication.
Q. To what is the grade of Companion limited?
A. To know the virtue of the first Elect man, his ambition, his fall, and his punishment.
Q. What is the age of the Companion?
A. A time fixed and limited.

END OF THE CATECHISM OF COMPANION ÉLU COËN

CATECHISM
OF PARTICULAR MASTER ÉLU COËN

Q. Are you a Master?
A. Yes, V.V.M., I am.
Q. By what will I know that you are a Master?
A. By my steps, the circumstances of my reception to the Mastership, and by my work in the circles of expiation.
Q. How have you been received Master?
A. By passing from the triangle to the circles.
Q. Why does the Master labor?
A. For the knowledge of the subdivision of the temporal terrestrial matter.
Q. What does this subdivision teach?
A. The knowledge of the three spiritous principles which compose the general terrestrial body, the celestial, and those of the permanent particular bodies on the surface of the earth.
Q. How have you been conducted to the Mastership?
A. As a villain that one leads to torture, sorrowfully vested, the cord at the neck, feet bare; in this position I have been admitted to my reception.
Q. Who has assisted you in your reception?
A. A Companion being who has sealed me with his name.
Q. Would you recognize him if you saw him?
A. Yes, Very Venerable Master.
Q. Oh good! Seek the Particular Master, he is among us!
Q. What is the number of the circles of expiation?
A. They are six in number.
Q. To what do these circles allude?
A. To the six powerful thoughts that the G.A. employed for the construction of his universal Temple.
Q. What have you observed of these six circumferences?
A. Four different mysterious branches, one of which is of palm, another of cedar, another of olive, and the other of willow.

Q. Have you observed nothing more?
A. I have observed a bowl of earth, a sea of bronze, and a flaming urn, as well as figures, characters, and innumerable lights.
Q. What do these four mysterious branches designate?
A. The branch of palm designates the power of the living God; that of cedar, the power of the God of life; that of olive, the power of the Spirit, and that of willow, the power of death or privation.
Q. What is designated by the bowl of earth, the sea of bronze, the flaming urn, the figures, the characters, and the innumerable lights that you have seen?
A. The bowl of earth designates the origin of my corporeal form, the water and the flaming urn the two principal elements which sustain it in its individuality, the figures and the characters designate the superior virtue of the different bodies superior to mine, and the number of lights designates the infinite number of spiritual agents who act in the Universal Temple.
Q. By whom have you been received Master?
A. By a Venerable Master of the Occident and two Surveillants.
Q. What do the three persons designate?
A. The V.M. designates the thought of the Creator; the First Surveillant, his action; and the Second Surveillant, his operation.
Q. How do the Particular Masters travel?
A. From the West to the North, to the South, and from there to the Orient by trembling steps.
Q. Why do the Particular Masters travel in this way?
A. To make allusion to the fact that every man is only here below in error and darkness.
Q. What are the attributes of a Particular Master?
A. The circle, the square, and the compass.
Q. What do these three things designate?
A. The circle designates the limits of the operations of the Particular Masters in the Order; the square, the perfection of their operations; and the compass, the route, and the conduct that they must keep in all their temporal and spiritual actions.
Q. What do the three columns of the Temple designate?

A. Three kinds of different mysterious branches of acacia.
Q. How do you distinguish them?
A. French acacia, grated acacia, and wild acacia.
Q. What do these three kinds of acacia designate?
A. The French acacia designates the spiritual Elect; the grafted, his disciples; and the wild designates the profane, impure, errants and vagabonds, the scandalous among the humans of Equity.
Q. What is the touch of recognition from one Particular Master to the other?
A. The circle between the square and the compass.
Q. What must a Particular Master observe?
A. Three things, which are charity, example, and perfect practice of the duties of the Order.
Q. What must he do?
A. Three things, which are the research into the knowledge of the sciences prohibited by divine law, to preserve himself from crass ignorance, and to never abuse his virtue of spiritual and corporeal material power in the Order...
Q. What is the essential number of a Particular Master?
A. The nonary number.
Q. What does this number designate?
A. Three things, which are the subjection of the Particular Master to the work of matter as being imperfect in the Order, the incertitude of his spiritual operations, temporal ones, and the reintegration of the principles of his corporeal individual.
Q. What is represented by the three candlesticks with three branches which enlighten the Particular Masters in their works?
A. The three different classes of spirits which direct and activate the General Terrestrial Temple, represented by the three degrees of the Class of the Porch.
Q. To what serves the Porch of our Temple?
A. To rough-hew and perfect the workers of the Order in order to employ them for the re-edification of the cult of the Creator, just as it was represented by that of the Temple of Solomon.

END OF THE CATECHISM OF THE PARTICULAR MASTER ÉLU COËN

CATECHISM
OF MASTER ÉLU COËN

Q. Are you a Master Élu Coën?
A. Yes, V.R. Master, I am and am made glory of the being.
Q. By what will I know that you are Élu [Elect]?
A. By the regularity of my entrance into the circle of reconciliation, by my operation, and by the power of my word.
Q. To what do the Master Élus work?
A. To the perpetual combat of the enemies of divine law and of those of the ordinary men of the earth.
Q. What is the attribute of the Master Élu?
A. The crossed globe, the dagger, and square.
Q. What is designated by the crossed globe, the dagger, and the square?
A. The crossed globe designates the sensible pain that all nature will endure, by the blows which were borne upon the person of the Elect beloved by the Creator, the sublime perfection of his virtue and of his powerful word, with which he has reconciled the earth with man and all with the Great Architect of the Universe.
Q. What is the decoration of the Master Élu?
A. The black band traced by five receptables, a globe, and a death's head surmounted by three daggers.
Q. What does this decoration signify?
A. The black band signifies the frightful dwelling of the men of matter, in which the perfect Master Élu has operated the reconciliation of the profane mortals; the five receptacles represent the four operations that the Divine Elect has operated in the four principal regions, and the fifth, the one that he has operated on behalf of his disciples, to the shame of the demons. The globe surmounted by three branches represents the satisfaction felt by the three different nations of the earth after their reconciliation, just as it had been represented to us by *Abraham*, *Isaac*, and *Jacob*; and the head surmounted by three

daggers represents the thought, action, and operation of the enemies of the Élus chosen by the divine power, just as it is well represented by the three nations that have each brought their blows upon the person of the perfect Master.

Q. How are these three nations named?

A. The Hebrew, the Galilean, and I will say nothing of the third.

Q. In what terrestrial regions do you admit these three nations?

A. The Hebrew to the east, the Galilean to the south, and the other to the north.

Q. What do the two broken columns represent?

A. The degradation of the power of the two corporized beings, represented by the two columns of the porch of the Temple, of which the one to the north represents the masculine body, and the one to the south represents the feminine body.

Q. What is represented by the two capitals detached from the two columns and overturned indistinctly on the ground?

A. The capitals detached from each of these columns alludes to the abandon and detachment that the Spirit, good conductor, has made from man, because of his prevarications, and leaves him to operate indifferently in error and darkness upon the surface of the earth.

Q. What is represented by the candlestick with nine branches which enlightens the Master Élus in the Order?

A. The nine different spiritual agents which operate and enlighten in the three temporal material regions, represented by the three different universal elements.

Q. What is your age in the capacity of Master Élu?

A. 3, 5, 6, 7, 4, and 8 years.

Q. To what alludes the number of age that you say you are in the capacity of Master Élu?

A. The number of age makes two allusions, the first to the various Divine spiritual operations that the perfect Master Élu has operated towards the Creator, on behalf of the universal nature; the second, to the number of time, which he has set to fulfill all his duties as man-God and divine among the humans.

Q. What are the essential numbers of the Master Élu?
A. 4, 7, and 8.
Q. To what alludes the quaternary number, the septenary, and the octonary?
A. The quaternary to the origin and the power of the Élu; the septenary to the powerful spiritual faculties that he has received from the Creator since his emancipation; and the octonary to the double power that the Élu, beloved of the Most High, had with him when he saw operated the reconciliation of the humans. By this example, every Master Élu may procure a similar property and virtue.
Q. At what hour does the Master Élu open the works?
A. At the ninth hour of the day.
Q. Why is that?
A. To allude to the ninth hour of the final three days when the reconciler finished all his temporal spiritual operations on behalf of the men of the earth.
Q. What did he do then?
A. He rendered the four powerful words that he had received from the G.A.O.T.U. at his destiny, after having consecrated them, for the manifestation of the divine glory and justice.
Q. What are these four words?
A. I am yet unaware, but they are represented to us by *Heli. Lama. Saba. Tanie.*
Q. At what hour does the Master Élu close the works?
A. At the third hour of the day.
Q. Why is that?
A. To allude to the retreat that the disciples of the perfect Master Élu took before the consummation of his operations.
Q. How were you placed at the time of your admission to the degree of Master Élu.
A. In a decent manner, but nevertheless the soul seized with fear.
Q. What reassured you?

A. The perfection of my operations, the justice of my actions, and the regular conduct that I have held in the order towards my brothers.

Q. In what position have you received the distinguished favor of Master Élu?

A. In a Temple regularly assembled by the divine spiritual thought, action, and operation, my body thrown down in three circumferences forming a perfect receptacle resting upon a double equilateral triangle, and aided by four circles of correspondence of operation for my reception.

Q. What was represented to you by all the things which have served at your reception as Master Élu?

A. The temple represents the place consecrated to the operations of the Master Élus, just as the perfect Master has designated it himself to his disciples by his operations made upon the general terrestrial temple; the three circles represent the three gifts that the perfect Master had given to his first disciples, which are admiration, understanding, and contemplation; the two bound triangles designate the origin of my body intimately bound with the general terrestrial one, the one and the other having the same triangular form; the receptacle, the destined place upon which is operated all things on behalf of humanity and the universality, just as every Divine spiritual thing is operated upon the body of the perfect Master before his death; the four circles of correspondence represent the spiritual inhabitants of the four different Celestial regions who have assisted spiritually with all the temporal spiritual operations that the Master has made in order to recall man to his first principle of temporal spiritual virtue, authority, and power.

Q. What characterizes you Master Élu?

A. The six authentic marks that I have received on the different parts of my body.

Q. Name them.

A. That of the head, the two hands, the feet, and towards the heart.

Q. What do these marks represent?
A. That of the head indicates to the heavens that his tribute has satisfied the justice of the Creator for his reconciliation; that of the left hand designates that which the inhabitants of the South still pay to the Divine justice; that of the right hand designates the tribute that the inhabitants of the northern terrestrial region have paid for their spiritual affiliation; those of the feet indicate the seal that the Creator had placed upon matter at the time of its undifferentiated state, in order to render it susceptible to retaining impressions on behalf of the different bodies which had to come out of it according to the will of the Creator; and that which is made upon the heart of the Master designates the power of the different spiritual agents that the Creator had marked by his invisible seal in order to cooperate with the spiritous essences of the first matter from where all the material and temporal bodies are emanated. It is from this that the first sages have professed the offering of the heart and soul to the Creator.
Q. What is represented by the three strikes of the dagger that the Master Élu gives upon the three different parts of his body, and the fourth upon the earth?
A. These three different blows designate: by the one that the Master Élu gives upon the throat, the renunciation that he makes of every species of science and other matter contrary to divine law, and to the permanent order in the East; the one that he gives upon the heart, indicating the South, explains the same subject as the first; the third that he gives upon the abdomen from the right side designating the Northern part, has the same relationship as the first two; and the fourth that he gives upon the earth designating the West has likewise the same significance as the first three.
Q. How are the four different renunciations represented to you?
A. By four different metals.
Q. Name them.
A. Lead, gold, iron, and copper.

Q. What do these four metals designate?
A. Lead, the condensation and gravity of matter; gold the sublimity of its spiritous essences; iron, the solidity of its virtue, and of the curse that the Creator placed reversible upon it after the prevarication of the first Elect man.
Q. [missing text - probably "How do the Master Élu travel?" – tans.]
A. In circumference formed by nine or by twenty-seven, by 27 steps in the form of a perfect square, and the sword in hand.
Q. Why do they travel with the sword in hand?
A. To remove every clandestine or profane being from their virtual and spiritual circumference, and in order to be able to be always ready to fight against the enemies of the Christian religion, those of the King, and those of the Order.
Q. What must a legitimate Master Élu observe?
A. Three things: exactitude on the discipline of the Order towards the brothers of the inferior class of the Porch; the regularity of their engagements in the Order; and perfect and humble obedience towards the principal chiefs of the Order.
Q. What must a Master Élu do?
A. Three things: the first, to withdraw from every clandestine society which treats and teaches apocryphal instructions, contrary to the divine spiritual law, and to the Order; second, every place of profanation and prostitution of spiritual things and of himself; and third to never withdraw himself from the Ordination that he has received, and to observe scrupulously the regimen of living in the Order according to what has been ordered to him by the perfect Master.
Q. What is designated by the square and compass strongly bound together?
A. The compass and square designate the intimate connection of the soul with the spirit represented by the conjunction of this figure.
Q. What is the name of the perfect Master Élu?
A. Hrlij in Hebrew, or Heli in the common language.

Q. What does this name signify?
A. Receptacle of the Divinity, or dedication of his own works.
Q. What is the name of the Temporal Master Élu?
A. Reaux in Hebrew, and Roux in the common tongue.
Q. What does this name signify?
A. Man-God of the Earth, raised above every temporal spiritual sense, upon which the glory and the justice of the Creator operates.
Q. Has the first Elect man always preserved the name of Reaux?
A. No, Very Respectable Master.
Q. Why is that?
A. The resolved ambition to raise his power above the One who had constituted him in virtue and authority, over every created creature, has placed him in a position to act contrary to his power, and by these means he has rendered ordinary man from invisible man that he had been.

END OF THE CATECHISM OF ÉLU

CATECHISM
OF THE
GRAND MASTER COËNS
CALLED GRAND ARCHITECT

Q. Are you a Grand Master Coëns?
A. Yes, Very Respectable Master, I am; and I glory in being this until the separation of my soul from my body.
Q. How have you been received Grand Master Coëns?
A. At the center of a brilliant light, assisted by four celestial regionary chiefs, represented by the four great Surveillants who were each placed in the center of each of the four circles of correspondence of the particular temple.
Q. At what age have you been received Grand Master Coën?
A. At the age of 80 years, which alludes to the eight years that I have consecrated in expiation in order to merit my ordination.
Q. How have you been ordained, and by whom have you operated?
A. By the thought and will of the Eternal and by the power, word, and intention of his deputies.
Q. Of what use have been the four regionary chiefs on behalf of your reception?
A. To remove and dissipate by their spiritual fires every species of imperfect being which would be able to pollute me.
Q. With what is the Grand Master Coën occupied?
A. With the purification of the material senses, to make them susceptible to participation in the various operations of the spirit.
Q. To what end does the Grand Master Coën labor?
A. To construct new Tabernacles and to rebuild the old ones, by the example of the ancient Grand Masters, to prepare them and make them suitable to receive within them the various words of power that govern and set in motion the different operations of every created being.

Q. How many types of Tabernacles are there in the Grand Universal Temple?
A. Four, and there may be no more.
Q. Name them.
A. Two material ones, represented by the particular bodies of man and woman; the third, the one that Moses constructed temporally; and the fourth is the temporal spiritual one, called the Sun, that the Great Architect of the Universe has destined to contain within it the temporal and spiritual names and sacred words of reaction distinguished by wisdom, flame of the temporal universal life.
Q. To what alludes the ark that Moses had constructed to rest in the Tabernacle that he had temporally constructed?
A. This ark is nothing but a repetition of what Noah had constructed, in which there were only material Tabernacles, in order to bear witness to the justice that was exercised upon the children of God, become the children of men by the covenant that they had made with the daughters of Cain.
Q. To what alludes, M.F., the ark that Noah had constructed?
A. It prophesied that which Moses has constructed to bring Israel out from the justice of the demons, to subject them to the conduct and justice of the Eternal; which is represented to us by the different animals that were put in the ark, and confirmed by the different nations that the ark of Moses has saved from the anger of the Creator. The brute animals may be considered to allude to the idolaters and the rational animals to the children of God.
Q. What means the name of Noah?
A. Saved from the waters.
Q. And that of Moses?
A. Issued from the waters.
Q. To what alludes the tabernacle that Moses had put at the center of the ark?
A. The ark being the true figure of the general terrestrial body, for the same reason, the Tabernacle is that which designates the

particular place where the Creator communicated with his first creature without being intermingled with the earth.

Q. Through whom has it been confirmed what we are told on this subject?

A. Through Moses, when he entered into the Tabernacle to communicate with the Eternal, to receive his orders, and to manifest them for the greater glory of the Divinity.

Q. Why did Moses always stand in front of the Tabernacle when he spoke to Israel?

A. As the Tabernacle was the place consecrated to be the deposit of all the divine, spiritual, temporal, material, and corporeal virtues and powers, he stood in this way to receive all the necessary intelligence in order to make a lasting impression upon Israel, with whom he wished to communicate by order of the Eternal.

Q. How many doors has this tabernacle?

A. Four, which alludes to the quadruple divine essence, to the four powers given to man, and to the four celestial regionary powers.

Q. Which are those upon which the Grand Master Coën has the right to knock and to open?

A. He has the right to knock on all four, but he only has the ability and the power to open that of the North and to close that of the South.

Q. Why does the Grand Master Coën not have the power to open all four, by the example of Moses who opened them as he willed?

A. Because the Grand Master Coën of our Order is yet only a temporal being, and may not have such power until he becomes, by the example of the first sages, a spiritual man.

Q. Since the tabernacle of Moses is a true representation of our material, in which part do we find the figure of the aforementioned doors?

A. At the head; as the most revealed part of our body, archetype of the thought, designating the door of the East; the power of hearing, given to the ear, designating the door of the North; contemplation, given to sight, designating the door of the South;

and the word, designating the door of the West, is given to the strength of the operation.

Q. To what alludes these four doors?

A. They allude to the four great principal chiefs operating the universe, figured again by the four great vats placed at the four corners of the Temple of Solomon.

Q. To what alludes these four great vats?

A. To the four great temporal priests who have operated the divine cult among humans and represented by the four Evangelists who have carried the various spiritual operations into the four quarters of the world.

Q. Who are the four principals who operate the universe?

A. Rhety under Adam, Enoch under the posterity of Seth, Melchizedek under the posterity of Abraham, and Christ on behalf of every created being.

Q. Who are the four high priests who have operated the divine cult among humans?

A. Zalmun among the Ishmaelites, Rharamoz among the Egyptians, Aaron among the Israelites, and Paul among the Christians.

Q. To what alludes the seven-branched candlestick of Moses?

A. To the seven celestial powers, to the seven spiritual gifts, to the seven operations that the Eternal manifested for the creation of this universe; which has been represented by the seven-branched candlestick which was placed in the Temple of Solomon and perpetuated unto us by the one which exists with the Romans.

Q. What is the power of the Grand Master Coën?

A. To paint, to trace all the emblems of the Order, when it will be demanded of him to offer the perfumes, to consecrate his fellow men into the circle of the Master Coëns, and to apply his powerful word to the four celestial regions and the three terrestrial, to keep careful watch over the ceremonial of the temporal spiritual operations.

Q. What is the qualification of the Grand Master Coëns?

A. Conductor of the holy ark and guardian of the doors of the Tabernacle.
Q. How long does the Grand Master Coën spend serving his Powerful Master?
A. Six days for the two equinoxes. Twelve days with the two solstices, fourteen days for the perfect operation of the two equinoxes, fourteen days for that of the two solstices, seven years for the perfect operation of reconciliation. 53=8.
Q. What is the faculty of the Grand Master Coën?
A. To operate their virtue and power, on Wednesday and Saturday of each week, all the months of the year, and in all perilous circumstances where the case requires them to operate their works and to impose their squared hands upon all things which are suitable to their operation.
Q. What are the circumstances of the reception of a Grand Master Coën?
A. Give them if the Grand Master requires it.
Q. At what hour are all the doors of the universal Tabernacle opened?
A. Although the times, days, months, and year be limited, we open them in all perilous circumstances of this life of tears.
Q. What is the sign of the Grand Master Coën?
A. Give it if it is ordered.
Q. What are the various words of power which consecrate him Grand Master Coën?
A. Give them likewise if it is ordered. 3, 4, 6, 7, 8, and 10, for the Powerful Master.
Q. To what alludes the powerful names and words which consecrate the Grand Master Coëns of our Order?
A. To those that the Creator gave to Moses, his Grand Master Coën, to make them reversible and to consecrate his fellow men to the divine spiritual operations.
Q. To what alludes the broken tablets of Moses and those which he brought down to the Israelites?

A. I am unaware, being left to the power of the one who is before me.

END OF THE CATECHISM OF G.M. COËN

CATECHISM
OF THE
GRAND ELECT OF ZOROBABEL
SO-CALLED KNIGHTS OF THE EAST

Q. Are you under the election of Zorobabel?
A. Yes, V.R.M., and the intimate covenant of Assyria with the unfortunate remainder of Israel is not unknown to me.
Q. Of what consists this covenant and to what does it allude?
A. This covenant consists of the freedom that Assyria has given to the tribes of Israel after the expiration of their captivity, which also alludes to the one that the Eternal will flee [make] with every created being after the expiration of time and their perfect reconciliation.
Q. By what are these things represented?
A. By the agreement that Zorobabel made with Cyrus and by the fruit of their operations which induced the King to lend every sort of relief to the tribes of Israel to whom he gave freedom despite all those who were opposed to it.
Q. And by whom are they confirmed to us?
A. By Christ and by his operations, of whom Zorobabel is the type, and his operations the type of every redemption; and those of Assyria opposing the freedom of Israel are the type of the iniquitous operations of the Hebrews when they opposed themselves to those of the Redeemer.
Q. What is the number of tribes who were in captivity in Babylon?
A. Judah, Benjamin, and a portion of Levi.
Q. Are you from any one of these tribes?
A. No, V.R.M., I am from the one that has always enjoyed its liberty.
Q. What do you call it?
A. Ephraim, the last of the Hebrews and the first of the Elect.

Q. How have you penetrated and understood the operations and the powerful agreement that Zorobabel had contracted with Cyrus in order to set Israel free, since you have never been in captivity?

A. By the intimate connection and the intimate relationship of correspondence that exists between all the spiritual and temporal operations of Zorobabel with those of ours which lets nothing escape our correspondence.

Q. At what age was Zorobabel subjugated in captivity?

A. From the age of seven years until that of seventy, which ended the captivity.

Q. At what age have you been received G. Elect of Zorobabel, among Israel, and what is your temporal age?

A. My temporal age is seventy years and that of my spiritual election is seven years.

Q. To what alludes the 77 years of which you enjoy in this lower world?

A. To the doubly powerful Spirit reigning in this lower world, represented by the double septenary character and represented by th perfect age of Zorobabel and by his spiritual reign.

Q. What is the duty of your election?

A. To combat my material passions in order to make them spiritual to vanquish the enemies of truth and those of liberty by the example of Zorobabel who has fought and conquered.

Q. In what place has the wise and peaceful Zorobabel fought and conquered?

A. At the passage of the formidable bridge of the river Starbuzarnai, which signifies passage of confusion, just as the counting of this name represents it to us as I explain it.

S 1, tar 2, bu 3, zar 4, nai 5.

Q. What are the different operations that Zorobabel has operated on behalf of Israel, at the time of its captivity?

A. Seven particulars and 70 annuals; the annual ones consisted of reminding the slaves of their first crime with their just punishment, with their expiation and their perfect reconciliation;

and the seven particulars inform these same slaves of their future liberty, of the different eras which have occurred in the past with Israel, those present, and all those which are to occur with it in the future.

Q. In what place has Zorobabel most manifested the 7 particular operations?

A. At the breaking of the six arches which formed the bridge of the said river and allowed the seventh one to remain without having damaged it.

Q. Why has Zorobabel broken the said arches, and what are the instruments he used for this operation?

A. I am unaware of them since those delivered have not had any knowledge of them.

Q. Why is that?

A. Because their material Temple has not been rebuilt, and because a sacrifice has not yet been made to the Creator.

Q. But, my brother, how is it possible for Zorobabel to have been able to destroy such a beautiful and magnificent bridge without the help of tools composed of metal, and to what alludes this operation and the seventh arch that he has left in all its perfection?

A. This event, V.R.M., ought not surprise us. By the example of the construction of the Temple of Solomon which was constructed without the help of tools composed of metal, Solomon had at his disposal the unknown workers who have cut the stones from the quarry; so why wouldn't we admit that Zorobabel had in his power those of material destruction?

Q. You have not spoken on the type of the seventh arch.

A. The seventh arch left in all its perfection alludes to the perfect existence of the spirit, which never exists entirely within the universe, but only through it; and all beings of form in this universe are only apparent beings, which must be promptly dissolved since they have been conceived in the imagination of the spirit, of which the forgotten arch is the image of perfect existence.

Q. Have you labored at the reconstruction of the Temple of Solomon?
A. No, V.R.M.
Q. Why is that?
A. By the strength of the opposing actions against this prophesied rebuilding by the multitude of those who oppose themselves to our passage of the river and to our freedom.
Q. What do these things explain?
A. That the rebuilding of this Temple was only the representation of that of our material Temple that the spirit must rebuild, not being within the power of man to perform a similar reconstruction.
Q. From where comes the name of Israel that you bear in preference to that of Hebrew, since you are children of Hebrew?
A. The name Israel shows the unique [iniquitous?] material operation that Jacob made in struggling against the spirit. Having succumbed to this operation, he was marked on the left leg, and his name of Jacob was changed into that of Israel, which means "strong against God" having sinned against the Spirit.
Q. What does the change of personal name represent to us?
A. This change of name prophesied the change of the Divine Law that the Eternal caused to come out of the Hebrews in order to pass it to the enemies of Israel, with whom it still resides.
Q. By whom has this event been predicted?
A. By Moses, when he broke the first tablets of Divine Law that he had received from the Creator on behalf of the Hebrews.
Q. The Hebrews have therefore never received any Divine Law through Moses?
A. Yes, V.R.M., they have received it from him, but it was not as complete as the first that he would have given them.
Q. How, my brother, do you distinguish that the law that Moses has given the Hebrews is not the same as the first?
A. Because the thought and hand of man has not been exercised in the first as it has been in the second.
Q. What does this event explain?

A. That Israel would remain purely under the ceremonial and conventional law, without power to operate the Divine Cult, the true law being taken out of their hands.
Q. To what alludes the veil that Moses placed over his face when he gave the second law to Israel?
A. This veil alludes to the veil that the spirit takes when it wishes to communicate with the one who beseeches it under a corporeal veil.
Q. Does this veil allude to anything else?
A. Yes, V.R.M., the veil confirms the veiled law that Israel has received from Moses; by the little confidence that they had in the power of the Eternal and of that of their leader.
Q. What is explained to us by the errant Hebrews and the law that they have ravished?
A. The errant Hebrews are the type of the error of the first converts, and the ravished law is that which will occur with all the men of the world who will be taken unawares of the cult of the divinity, and they will be spiritual errants, just as Israel is in the Temporal.
Q. What is the number of power of the Elect of Zorobabel?
A. 3, 7, 8, which allude to the terrestrial spiritual power, to that of the temporal spiritual, and to the double divine spiritual power.
Q. What is the genre of operations of the Elect of Zorobabel?
A. The *water*, the *earth*, and the *fire*.
Q. At what hour do they open their works?
A. All seven months, on the seventh day of the first quarter of the moon, which is from the seventh day of the first quarter of the moon of March until the seventh day of the first quarter of the moon of October, time when Israel received the second law, and came out of the towns of Egypt.
Q. By whom have you been consecrated Elect of Zorobabel?
A. By the double power and by that of *Zoroal* and of *Zoroael*, his two spiritual associates.
Q. Explain to us, my brother, the names of the three persons who have consecrated you to this august dignity.

A. *Zorobabel*, called enemy of confusion; *Zoroal*, enemy of matter; Zoroael, protector of miners and friend of wisdom.
Q. What is your rank?
A. Friend of God, protector of virtue, and professor of truth.

END OF THE CATECHISM OF THE CHIEFS OF THE ORIENT

END NOTES

1. Let us make note of this sentence of a judge who recognized the validity of a secret tribunal. As stroke of morality, it is rather curious and we could not boast ourselves in our era such a liberalism.
2. This passage is precious, for it shows, though counter to the opinion of nearly all the critics, that Martinès was Catholic and not Israelite. The words "my religion" indicate furthermore that there had not been a conversion.
3. Lusignan.
4. See *the Treaté élémentaire de Magie pratique.*
5. See *Traité élémentare de Magie Pratique* (3rd part).
6. Franck, *op. cit.*, p. 35.
7. This is the only time in his letters that Martinès speaks of these mysterious "predecessors" from whom he holds his doctrine.
8. See on this subject the same teaching given in China by the mystical triangle.
(*Traité meth. des Sciences occultes*, p. 921.)
9. Wronski lays out with even more details the same idea in his *Messianisme.*

10. Amiable and Colfavru, *La Franc-Maconnerie au XVIIIe siècle.*
11. See Ragon, Orthodoxie Mac., p. 56.
12. Amiable and Colfavru, op. cit.
13. Certain authors even claim that the internment of Louis XVI at the Temple was the result of the decision of the brethren of the Templar rite.
14. Mounier. - *De l'influence attribuée aux francs-macons dans la Révolution francaise*, 155 and 156.

www.ingramcontent.com/pod-product-compliance
Lightning Source LLC
Chambersburg PA
CBHW022011160426
43197CB00007B/375

* 9 7 8 0 9 9 7 3 1 0 1 6 0 *